A TREATISE

ON

SELF-KNOWLEDGE,

BY JOHN MASON, A.M.

—— E cœle descendit γνωθι σεαυτον.—Juv.

The proper study of mankind is man.—Pope.

TO WHICH IS PREFIXED

A BRIEF MEMOIR OF THE AUTHOR.

New-York:
PUBLISHED BY LANE & SCOTT,
200 Mulberry-street.
JOSEPH LONGKING, PRINTER.
1851.

PREFACE.

We consider Mason on Self-Knowledge one of the best books which we have ever read. It was our good fortune to fall in with an old copy of this work early in our ministerial course, and the impressions which its perusal left upon the tablet of our heart are not yet erased. We have uniformly recommended it, especially to the young, as eminently adapted to prepare the mind for efforts in the pursuit of various knowledge. If we are ignorant of ourselves, what else can we know to any good purpose? And in our efforts to acquire this knowledge, I am persuaded, no book, except the Bible, will render us more effective aid. Its great practical principles should be deeply impressed upon the mind of the Christian, the scholar, and the man of business. The teacher of religion especially should become perfectly familiar with them.

In preparing the present edition, it has been our object to give it to the reader in as perfect a form as possible. We have consequently used two different editions, and have availed ourselves of the excellences of both. We have retained the notes in their appropriate places as inserted by the author, which, by some editors, have been thrown into an appendix, and by others omitted altogether. We have also left the text perfect, which in some editions is mutilated: thus giving to the public an edition of the work more complete than any which has been issued, either in Europe or in this country, in modern times.

The author, in a few instances, proceeds upon philosophical principles which are now exploded. Such passages we have not scrupled to retain, presuming that the intelligent reader will recollect the period in which he lived, and, moreover, that these principles are not at all essential to the general scope of his argument. We preferred this course to printing the work in a state of mutilation, which would make it appear like a work of more recent date than the times of the author. If the writers of the last century are defective in some branches of learning, they are not barren of *thought*, a commodity not always so abundant in the authors of our own time as to surfeit their readers. We would by no means undervalue the improvements of the present age in physical and mental philosophy; but we are free to confess, that we would, in some instances, readily exchange a considerable portion of these for a tithe of the intellectual and moral power wielded by the giants of the preceding century. We love the old English authors, and we would not lay hands upon the venerable monuments of their piety and learning without the utmost necessity. With these explanations, we now put this invaluable treasure into the hands of the reader, most devoutly praying that it may be made to him a present and an eternal blessing.

George Peck.

December 11, 1842.

CONTENTS.

PART I.

PART II.

PART III.

AN

ACCOUNT OF THE LIFE

OF THE

REV. JOHN MASON, A. M.

THE Rev. John Mason, author of the ensuing Treatise on Self-Knowledge, was born at Dunmow, in Essex, in the year 1705–6. His father was a dissenting minister, and was, we apprehend, successively pastor to congregations at Daventry in Northamptonshire; Dunmow in Essex; and at Spaldwick in Lincolnshire, at which last place he died, and was buried in the year 1722–3. This gentleman had a brother, the Rev. William Mason, a clergyman in the established Church, who, in the latter part of his life, held two livings, of which one was in Buckinghamshire, and the other in Derbyshire.* They were the children

* From this circumstance a gentleman, who about five years ago had thoughts of presenting to the public an account of his relation, the author of Self-Knowledge, suspected that he was

of the Rev. John Mason, A. M., who held the rectory of Water-Stratford, in the county of Bucks, and well known as author of a little posthumous work, published by his grand-son,

a branch of the same family from which the Rev. William Mason, a well-known and excellent poet, was descended. He made the inquiry, and received, in reply, the following letter:—

"*Aston, April* 3, 1797.

"SIR,—I am sorry that I can trace in the simple annals of my ancestry nothing which can afford me any ground for claiming either a direct or collateral relationship with Mr. John Mason of Cheshunt, who I believe to have been an excellent Christian moralist, and whom, therefore, I should have been more proud of owning for one of my family, than if he had had part of the *blood of all the Howards.* My table of genealogy goes no higher than to Valentine Mason, clerk, who was born, as I suppose, in the latter part of the reign of Elizabeth, as I find from Torre's MSS. in the cathedral at York, which are held authentic documents; that he resigned the vicarage of Driffield, a very small living, (of which, as precentor of York, I am now patron,) in 1623, for that of Elloughton in the same east riding of Yorkshire, (one I believe, at that time, little more valuable,) where he died in 1639. He had three sons and three daughters; two of the sons, I believe, succeeded in trade at Kingston-upon-Hull, and the third, William, was brought up to the Church, and had the living of Wensley, near Richmond, in the north riding, who left a landed estate in various parishes in the east riding, of which, as the last male heir, I am now possessed, and with me the family name will be extinct. I have a paper of my grandfather's, Hugh Mason, who was collector of the customs at the port of Hull, which informs me that Valentine Mason descended, as a younger brother, from a Mason of Cheriton, alias Cherington, in Oxfordshire. But the truth of this (though and recommended by Dr. Watts, entitled, "Select Remains," &c., &c. In the preface to this work, the author is represented as a person of as eminent a character in the religious world as most ages have produced, and though by principle a conformist to the established Church of England, yet he was very far from cherishing a bitter spirit againt dissenters, or such as

I tried by a friend in that county) I could not ascertain, and I believe it was merely founded on the same arms which all the Masons, as well as the Masons in France, bear, viz., a lion bifronted azure on a shield Or. You will, I hope, pardon me for giving you all these genealogical notices, as it is merely to show you that all I know of my family is bounded within the precincts of Yorkshire, and therefore I can claim no alliance with one seated in Essex or Buckinghamshire.

"Though you speak much too highly of my poetical productions, your panegyric claims my thanks, which I herewith give you, and subscribe myself, with due regard, sir,

"Your very much obliged and obedient servant,

"W. Mason.

"*John Mason Good, Esq., Guilford-street.*"

It has been thought proper to preserve the whole letter, as it is highly probable that it was the last Mr. Mason ever wrote. It is dated April the 3d, 1797: on that very day, in consequence of a slight contusion which had previously happened as he was getting into his carriage, a mortification ensued, which in forty-eight hours put a period to his life. "The character," says his biographer, "with which he ought to be handed down to posterity, is that of a man virtuous in his morals, amiable in his manners, and ornamental in the republic of letters." *See the Annual Necrology for* 1797–8.

differed from him in opinion. He died at Water-Stratford in the county of Bucks, A. D. 1694, having been rector of that place twenty years. His fervour of spirit in the cause of God and religion was uncommon. His learning was considerable, his capacity above the common level, and his application extraordinary.

We have not been able to ascertain to whom the subject of this memoir was indebted for the earlier part of his education; but he pursued his academical studies as a candidate for the ministry under the Rev. and learned John Jennings, who presided at a very respectable seminary at Kibworth in Leicestershire about the year 1719, and afterward removed to Hinckley in the same county. When he had finished his studies, he became chaplain and private tutor in the family of Governor Feaks, at his seat near Hatfield. He could not have remained very long in this situation, as, in the year 1729–30, he accepted an invitation to the pastoral charge of a congregation at Dorking in Surry. It was not till after Mr. Mason had resided ten years at Dorking that he became known to the public as an author. His first piece was a sermon, published at the desire of those who heard it, entitled, "Subjection to the Higher Powers," preached November 5,

1740. In the year 1743 he published, without his name, a tract, entitled, "A Plain and Modest Plea for Christianity, or a Sober and Rational Appeal to Infidels," &c., which was well received and much read, and through the medium of Dr. Walker, formerly tutor to an academy at Mile End, it procured for the author, unsought for, the degree of A. M. from Edinburgh. His "Treatise on Self-Knowledge" was published in the year 1745, a work which has already passed through many editions, and which has been esteemed by able and impartial judges as one of the most useful treatises on practical piety that ever was written in the English, or perhaps in any language. It has been taken up as a book fit and proper to be distributed among the poor, who are unable to procure books at their own expense, by several societies, both among dissenters and persons adhering to the established Church. It has not been confined to the language in which it was written, but has been translated and circulated in several countries on the continent.

At Dorking Mr. Mason continued till July the 6th, 1746, where he was held in high estimation both as a preacher and a friend. To his hearers, he was able, at the close of seventeen years' ministry, to appeal for their testimony to the sincerity and earnestness of his labours in the cause in which he appears to have engaged from his heart. "During the whole course of my preaching among you," says he in his farewell discourse, "I have avoided controversial subjects as much as possible; that is, as far as is consistent with ministerial fidelity. And those that I have handled were mostly such as were of the greatest importance to common Christianity; which I have always endeavoured to treat in the plainest manner I could. But my chief aim hath been to affect your minds and my own with a deeper sense of those great, uncontroverted principles of Christianity which enter into the very essence of religion, and without an habitual regard to which, our profession of it, and that of every party, is vain. For I have often thought, it is much more necessary to endeavour to mend the heart than stuff the head. And that Christians in general have more need to have their spirits improved, than their understandings informed; and want more zeal rather than more light; better tempers rather than better notions: and that a bad heart with right notions is much worse than a good heart with wrong notions; for if the heart be wrong, it matters little that the head is right."

Then, after recapitulating the principal duties incumbent upon them as Christians, and which at all times he had sedulously recommended as of prime importance, he concludes in the following words :—

" God is my witness, and so are you, that I never affected to warp your minds to party notions, to amuse you with empty speculations, to move you with vehement address, to please you with the jingling ornaments of style, or win you with the studied arts of speech; my aim hath been to make my way to your hearts, by opening and inculcating to you, in the plainest and most unartful manner, those great and important truths which have first affected my own. What hath been my success, God knows: and what my fidelity. May he graciously forgive the defects both of preacher and hearers! before whom we must both another day appear to answer for them. And O! may we all find mercy of him in that day!

" And now, my dear Christian friends and brethren, farewell. I now take my final leave of you for ever as your minister and pastor. For all the instances of your affection and friendship, I heartily thank you. Wherein any of you have been defective in your regard to me as your minister, I heartily forgive you;

wherein I have been defective in my duty to you as my people, I heartily ask forgiveness. And may the God of all mercy forgive, accept, direct, and bless us all; and preserve us to that happy world, where we shall meet to part no more!"

At this period Mr. Mason, upon the invitation of a large and respectable congregation of dissenters, removed to Cheshunt in Hertfordshire, where he spent the remainder of his days, as a very useful preacher. Nor was he less known as an author. During his residence at Cheshunt his publications were numerous and respectable, of the principal of which we shall here give an account.

His largest work is entitled the "Lord's Day Evening Entertainment," in four volumes, containing fifty-two sermons, which he offered to the public as a "complete set of practical discourses for the use of families, recommending and urging the great and substantial points of Christianity in a plain and striking manner, and free from all distinguishing peculiarities in style and sentiments." The second edition of this work, which has been popular in families, was published in the year 1754.

In the year 1758 he published, in one volume, fifteen discourses, devotional and practical, together with an historical dissertation on the analogy between the behaviour of God's people toward him, in the several periods of the Jewish and Christian church, and his correspondent dispensations toward them in those respective periods. The design of this dissertation is to show, that however ready we may be to censure and condemn the temper and behaviour of the Jews, yet that the conduct of Christians has been very much the same, in the several periods of the Christian church: and to point out some remarkable instances of analogy between the dealings of Providence toward them, and his dispensations toward us; in consequence of that similarity between their conduct and ours. Our author has in this essay shown an extensive and accurate knowledge of ancient and modern history, and a considerable degree of critical acumen in pointing out the various analogies which subsist between the different histories; he has rendered the whole highly interesting by the insertion of a great variety of historical and biographical facts, especially those which relate to the first reformers.

In the year 1761 Mr. Mason published his "Christian Morals," in two volumes. The object of the author in these excellent discourses was, he tells us, to moderate the zeal of Christians for their several party distinctions, and to recall their attention to the acknowledged importance of those indisputed principles, without the practical influence of which no man can be a Christian, and all the good sense, and all the orthodoxy in the world will avail him nothing. "O," says he, "did deep humility, divine love, fervent faith, and heartfelt charity, but once shed their heavenly influence in our souls; how soon should we learn to despise that light chaff of mystic or minute subtleties in divinity which some are so fond of, and to bend all our cares and efforts, in dependance on divine grace, to cultivate in ourselves those holy dispositions, which constitute all our happiness, both in this world and for ever.

"To contribute somewhat to this great end, I have once more cast in my mite, as what I judged to be of the greatest service I am capable of doing the cause and gospel of Christ, while I live."

To the second volume of these discourses is added a sermon on the death of George II.—"A king," says our author, "whose memory will be ever dear to all the friends of truth, moderation, and the Protestant religion." This and some other discourses on political occasions exhibit in the writer a true patriot, and friend to the British constitution as settled at the revolution. Of the tories of that day, and those who would have brought in the detested race of the Stewarts, he says, "They who were most clamorous for non-resistance under the worst government, were always the most forward to oppose the best."

Next to the "Treatise on Self-Knowledge," our author's most popular work is entitled, "The Student and Pastor, or directions how to attain to eminence and usefulness in those respective characters." These directions contain useful and salutary advice as to the management of time; the best mode of reading and studying; of improving by conversation and reflection; of composing sermons, and of administering in all the public services of religion: the last chapter of the work respects the difficulties which a minister may expect to meet with in the execution of his office, and his proper support and encouragement under them.

About the year 1749, or '50, Mr. Mason published "An Essay on Elocution, intended chiefly for the assistance of those who instruct others in the art of reading, and of those who are called to speak in public," which was received with great approbation, and in the course of a few years went through three impressions, and may be considered as the foundation of many of our public popular essays on the same subject. It was originally published without the name of the author, and met, in that state, with considerable encouragement and patronage at one of our public universities; but when Mr. Mason claimed it as his own, by prefixing his name to the second edition, that learned body is said to have scouted it from their walls as the work of a dissenter.

On similar subjects we have "Essays on Poetical and Prosaic Numbers and Elocution;" and "An Essay on the Power and Harmony of Prosaic Numbers." These tracts were well received by the public: of the former the author says, "I am sensible that my attempts to elucidate the power of numbers, both in poetry and prose, are far from going to the bottom of that curious and delightful subject, but if they are not deemed quite superficial, it is enough: they were never designed for profound and elaborate disquisitions. In short, they pretend to no more than what their titles express, essays to illustrate the first principles of *that* science which greatly engaged the attention of the ancient orators, but which has unaccountably fallen into so much neglect by the moderns."

In the year 1761 Mr. Mason collected these several essays, and published them together in a small octavo volume. This, we apprehend, is the last edition of them; but they are now, and have been for many years, exceedingly scarce, and rarely to be met with in catalogues.

Notwithstanding the various and important engagements of Mr. Mason as an author and pastor of a large congregation, he found time for the education of several young gentlemen for the ministry; among these were the Rev. Mr. Stanshall, late of Chertsea, to whom, in the year 1753, he addressed "A Letter to a Friend upon his Entrance on the Ministerial Office;" which contains directions to a minister with regard to his personal conduct, his private studies, and his public ministrations; and the Rev. John Somersett, who was some years settled as pastor to a congregation at Chipping Ongar, in Essex, and who died in the year 1780. The course of polemical lectures which Mr. Mason read to his pupils were printed in the Protestant Magazine for the years 1794, 1795, and 1796.

After a life devoted to the attainment and diffusion of useful knowledge, Mr. Mason died

February 10th, 1763, in the fifty-eighth year of his age. As a Christian minister, his time had been very equally divided between the congregations at Dorking and Cheshunt, a circumstance which he particularly noticed to a friend and relation while he was on his dying pillow, and which he seems to have anticipated in the preface to his farewell sermon preached at Dorking. "Great," says he, "is my esteem, and great my affection for you; and therefore great my concern at leaving you. There is but *one* scene more moving that I expect to go through, and that is, leaving the world. And then all the varying scenes of providence which are apt to fill our minds with grief and heaviness will be for ever at an end."

His last illness was occasioned by a cold caught in visiting one of his congregation, who lived at the distance of about two miles from Cheshunt. Before he could return to his own house, he, and a friend that accompanied him, were surrounded in a fog and mist. Mr. Mason complained of a general chilliness, and never after that day went out of his house. He left behind him a widow, the daughter of the Rev. James Waters, of Uxbridge, but no child to exhibit a father's virtues, or emulate his example.

He was buried in the church-yard of Cheshunt, where there is the following inscription to his memory:—

Here rests all that was mortal
of the late Rev., learned, and pious
JOHN MASON, A. M.,
who was Minister to the
congregation of
Protestant Dissenters in this parish 17 years.
He ceased from his labours,
and was called to receive his reward,
Feb. 10, 1763, aged 58 years.
"Be followers of them who through faith and
patience inherit the promises."

The character and general habits of Mr. Mason, as given by a surviving friend, together with what is said of him in a sermon preached by the Rev. John Hodge, on occasion of his death, will properly conclude the memoirs of a man respecting whom little is now known to the public.

As to his general habits and mode of life, he was as regular and uniform as any man I ever knew; he was not an early riser in the morning, being seldom up till about eight o'clock. After prayers, and reading a portion of the Scriptures, he breakfasted, then smoked his pipe, reading at the same time the newspaper, or some modern publication. He then retired to his study, where he spent the whole of the morning, except about an hour before dinner, which he usually devoted to walking or riding. After dinner he enjoyed his pipe and friend in a cheerful and easy manner: and either in his own family, with a select party of friends, or abroad in the society of some of his congregation, with whom he was in high estimation, he spent the remainder of the day. He was free, easy, communicative, and pleasant in conversation, and much of the gentleman appeared in all his behaviour. His acquaintance was much sought after, and he himself took great delight in society. He was one of the association of ministers for Essex and Hertfordshire, and was an ornament to it, though, an account of the liberality of his religious sentiments, one or two withdrew. His religious opinions were of the moderate kind, he was an enemy to controversy, and a friend to peace. Though abused by some, for want of knowing him better, and destitute themselves of the Christian temper and charity, he never returned railing, but submitted to the unjust contumely from a consciousness of the integrity of his heart. His sermons were correct, clear, nervous, and always illustrative of the text and doctrine he had chosen to explain; they were ever adapted to promote the purposes of piety and charity. "His religion," says Mr. Hodge, "appears to me to have been thoroughly catholic, and therein truly Christian. While he himself, from principle, adhered to the cause of Protestant non-conformity, amidst all its present discouragements, as apprehending it to have the nearest connection with the cause of truth, and liberty, and serious godliness, still he kept himself at the greatest distance from every thing of a narrow party spirit, by confining Christianity to his own particular communion; on the contrary, he was free to converse with others as with Christian brethren, ready to discern and acknowledge real merit, and esteem true learning and piety wherever he met with it.

"His removal from us (so it pleased unerring Wisdom to appoint) was after no long previous confinement, but of few days at most; during which, and under all the pains with which he had then to struggle, his mind appeared remarkably serene and composed: not a single murmuring, hardly a complaining word, was ever heard from him. As, through the goodness of an indulgent Providence, he retained the use of his reasoning powers to the last, so he was found to the last calm and resigned; his end truly was peace.

"Providence hath taken him away in the midst of his days and usefulness; when, considering only his age and the apparent vigour of his constitution, his continued life, and further usefulness in the church of God, might have been with reason hoped for through many future years. But the supreme Lord of life and death hath done his pleasure; and it is your duty, Christians, to submit and adore."

In the pulpit he was grave and solemn. His voice was clear, his delivery deliberate, distinct, and void of all affectation. He used little or no action; but he was esteemed a pleasing preacher, because his manner was easy and natural. His sentences were concise, and he never studied length, or the art of protracting his discourses, so as to tire the people: he had rather, as he was accustomed to say, and according to his directions in the "Student and Pastor," "leave them longing than loathing."

PREFACE.

THE subject of the ensuing Treatise is of great importance; and yet I do not remember to have seen it cultivated with that exactness, perspicuity, and force, with which many other moral and theological themes have been managed. And, indeed, it is but rarely that we find it particularly and fully recommended to us, in a set and regular discourse, either from the pulpit or the press. This consideration, together with a full persuasion of its great and extensive usefulness, hath put me upon an endeavour, in this manner, to render it more familiar to the minds of Christians.

Mr. Baxter, indeed, has a treatise professedly upon this subject, entitled, *The Mischief of Self-Ignorance, and the Benefit of Self-Acquaintance;* and I freely acknowledge some helps I received from him: but he hath handled it (according to his manner) in so lax and diffuse a way, introducing so many things into it that are foreign from it, omitting others that properly belong to it, and skimming over some with a too superficial notice, that I own I found myself much disappointed in what I expected from him, and was convinced that there wanted something more correct, nervous, and methodical, to be written on this subject.

I am far from having the vanity to think, that this, which I now offer to the public, is entirely free from those faults which I have remarked in that pious and excellent author; and I am sensible, that, if I do not fall under a much heavier censure myself, it must be owing to the great candour of my reader, which he will be convinced I have some title to, if he but duly consider the nature and extent of the subject. For it is almost impossible to let the thoughts run freely upon so copious and comprehensive a theme, in order to do justice to it, without taking too large a scope in some particulars that have a near affinity to it, as I fear I have done, (part i, chap. 14,) concerning the knowledge, guard, and government of the thoughts.

But there is a great difference between a short, occasional, and useful digression, and a wide rambling from the subject, by following the impulse of a luxuriant fancy. A judicious taste can hardly excuse the latter, though it may be content the author should gather a few flowers out of the common road, provided he soon returns into it again.

Which brings to my mind another thing, which, I am sure, I have great reason to crave the reader's patience and pardon for, (the best end I know of prefaces,) and that is, the free use I have made of some of the ancient heathen writers in my marginal quotations,* which, I own, looks like an ostentation of reading, which I always abhorred. But it was conversing with those authors that first turned my thoughts to this subject. And the good sense I met with in most of their aphorisms and sentiments, gave me an esteem for them; which made it difficult for me to resist the temptation of transcribing several of them, which I thought pertinent to the matter in hand. But, after all, I am ashamed to see what an old-fashioned figure they make in the margin. However, if the reader thinks they will too much interrupt the course of the subject, he may entirely omit them: though, by that means, he will perhaps lose the benefit of some of the finest sentiments in the book.

I remember a modern writer I have very lately read is grievously offended with Mr. Addison for so much as mentioning the name

* In many editions of this valuable work the "quotations" here referred to are omitted—in this, however, they are inserted.—*Am. Editor.*

of Plato, and presuming, in one of his Spectators, to deliver his notions of humour in a kind of allegory, after the manner of that Greek author; which he calls a "formal method of trifling, introduced under a deep ostentation of learning, which deserves the severest rebuke;" and, perhaps, a more severe one was never given upon so small a provocation. From gentlemen of so refined and very nice a taste, I can expect no mercy. But the public is to judge whether this be not as culpable and nauseous an affectation as the contrary one, which prevailed so much in the last century.

One great view I had in mine eye when I put these thoughts together, was the benefit of youth, and especially those of them that are students and candidates for the sacred ministry; for which they will find no science more immediately necessary (next to a good acquaintance with the word of God) than that which is recommended to them in the following Treatise; to which every branch of human literature is subordinate, and ought to be subservient. For, certain it is, the great end of philosophy, both natural and moral, is to know ourselves, and to know God. "The highest learning is to be wise, and the greatest wisdom is to be good;" as Marcus Antoninus somewhere observes.

It has often occurred to my mind, in digesting my thoughts upon this subject, what a pity it is that this most useful science should be so generally neglected in the modern methods of education ; and that preceptors and tutors, both in public and private seminaries of learning, should forget, that the forming the manners is more necessary to a finished education than furnishing the minds of youth. Socrates thought so, who made *all* his *philosophy* subservient to morality; and took more pains to rectify the tempers, than replenish the understanding, of his pupils; and looked upon all knowledge as useless speculation that was not brought to this end, to make the person a wiser or a better man. And without doubt, if, in the academy, the youth has once happily learned the great art of managing his temper, governing his passions, and guarding his foibles, he will find a more solid advantage from it in after life, than he could expect from the best acquaintance with all the systems of ancient and modern philosophy.

It was a very just and sensible answer which Agesilaus, the Spartan king, returned to one who asked him, what that was in which youth ought principally to be instructed? He replied, "That which they will have most need to practise when they are men." Were this single rule but carefully attended to in the method of education, it might probably be conducted in a manner much more to the advantage of our youth than it ordinarily is. For, as Dr. Fuller observes, "that pains we take in books or arts which treat of things remote from the use of life, is but a busy idleness." And what is there in life which youth will have more frequent occasion to practise than this? What is there which they afterward more regret the want of? What is there in which they want a greater help and assistance than the right government of their passions and prejudices? And what more proper season to receive those assistances, and to lay a foundation for this difficult, but very important science, than the early part of youth?

It may be said, "It is properly the office and care of parents to watch over and correct the tempers of their children in the first years of their infancy, when it may easily be done;" but if it be not effectual then, (as it very seldom is,) there is the more necessity for it afterward. But the truth is, it is the proper office and care of all who have the charge of youth, and ought to be looked upon as the most important and necessary part of education

It was the observation of a great divine and reformer, that "he who acquires his learning at the expense of his morals, is the worse for his education." And we may add that he who does not improve his temper, together with his understanding, is not much the better for it; for he ought to measure his progress in science by the improvement of his morals; and remember, that he is no further a learned man, than he is a wise and good man; and that he cannot be a finished philosopher till he is a Christian.

But whence is it, that moral philosophy, which was so carefully cultivated in the ancient academy, should be forced in the modern to give place to natural, that was originally designed to be subservient to it? which is to exalt the handmaid into the place of the mistress; which appears not only a preposterous, but a pernicious method of instruction: for, as the mind takes a turn of future life, suitable to the tincture it hath received in youth, it will naturally conclude, that there is no necessity to regard, or, at least, to lay any stress upon those things which were never inculcated upon it as things of importance then; and so will grow up in a neglect or disesteem of those things which are more necessary to make a person a wise and truly understanding man, than all those rudiments of science he brought with him from the school or the college.

It is really a melancholy thing to see a young gentleman of shining parts and a sweet disposition, who has gone through the common course of academical studies, come out into the world under an absolute government of his passions and prejudices ; which have increased with his learning, and which, when he comes to be better acquainted with human life, and human nature, he is soon sensible and ashamed of; but perhaps is never able to conquer as long as he lives, for want of that assistance which he ought to have received in his education; for a wrong education is one of those three things to which it is owing (as an ancient Christian philosopher justly observes) that so few have the right government of their passions.

I would not be thought to disparage any part of human literature ; but should be glad to see this most useful branch of science, the knowledge of the heart, the detecting and correcting hurtful prejudices, and the right government of the temper and passions, in more general esteem, as necessary at once to form the gentleman, the scholar, and the Christian.

And if there be any thing in the following sheets which may be helpful to students, who have a regard to the right government of their minds, while they are furnishing them with useful knowledge, I would particularly recommend them to their perusal.

I have nothing further to add, but to desire the reader's excuse for the freedom with which I have delivered my sentiments in this matter, and for detaining him so long from the subject of the ensuing Treatise, which I now leave to his candid and serious thoughts, and the blessing of Almighty God to make it useful to him.

A TREATISE

ON

SELF-KNOWLEDGE.

PART I.

CHAPTER I.

The nature and importance of the subject.

A DESIRE of knowledge is natural to all human minds; and nothing discovers the true quality and disposition of the mind more, than the particular kind of knowledge it is most fond of.

Thus we see that low and little minds are most delighted with the knowledge of trifles, as in children; an indolent mind, with that which serves only for amusement, or the entertainment of the fancy; a curious mind is best pleased with facts; a judicious, penetrating mind, with demonstration and mathematical science; a worldly mind esteems no knowledge like that of the world: but a wise and pious man, before all other kinds of knowledge, prefers that of God and his own soul.

But some kind of knowledge or other the mind is continually craving after, and after a further proficiency in: and, by considering what kind of knowledge it most of all desires, its prevailing turn and temper may easily be known.

This desire of knowledge, like other affections planted in our natures, will be very apt to lead us wrong, if it be not well regulated. When it is directed to improper objects, or pursued in an improper manner, it degenerates into a vain and criminal curiosity. A fatal instance of this in our first parents we have upon sacred record, the unhappy effects of which are but too visible in all.

Self-knowledge is the subject of the ensuing Treatise; a subject which, the more I think of, the more important and extensive it appears: so important, that every branch of it seems absolutely necessary to the right government of the life and temper; and so extensive, that the nearer view we take of the several branches of it, the more are still opening to the view, as necessarily connected with it as the other. Like what we find in microscopical observations on natural objects, the better the glasses, and the nearer the scrutiny, the more wonders we explore; and the more surprising dicoveries we make of certain properties, parts, or affections belonging to them, which were never before thought of. In order to a true self-knowledge, the human mind, with its various powers and operations, must be narrowly inspected; all its secret springs and motives ascertained; otherwise our self-acquaintance will be but partial and defective; and the heart after all will deceive us. So that in treating of this subject there is no small danger, either of doing injury to it, by a slight and superficial examination on the one hand, or of running into a research too minute and philosophical for common use on the other. These two extremes I shall keep in my eye, and endeavour to steer a middle course between them.

"Know thyself" is one of the most useful and comprehensive precepts in the whole moral system. And it is well known in how great a veneration this maxim was held by the ancients; and how highly the duty of self-examination was esteemed as necessary to it.

Thales, one of the seven wise men of Greece, is said to have been the first author of it. He used to say, that for a man to know himself is the hardest thing in the world. It was then adopted by Chilo, another of the seven sages, and is one of the three precepts which Pliny affirms to have been consecrated at Delphos in golden letters. It was afterward greatly admired, and frequently adopted by others, till at length it acquired the authority of a divine oracle; and was supposed to have been given originally by Apollo himself. Of which general opinion Cicero gives us this reason; "because it hath such a weight of sense and wisdom in it as appears too great to be attributed to any man." And this opinion, of its coming originally from Apollo himself, perhaps was the reason that it was written in golden capitals over the door of his temple at Delphos.

And why this excellent precept should not be held in as high esteem in the Christian world as it was in the heathen, is hard to conceive. Human nature is the same now as it was then: the heart as deceitful; and the necessity of watching, knowing, and keeping it the same. Nor are we less assured that this precept is divine: nay, we have a much greater assurance of this than they had; they supposed it came down from heaven, we know it did; what they conjectured, we are sure of. For this sacred oracle is dictated to us in a manifold light, and explained to us in various views, by the Holy Spirit, in that revelation which God hath been pleased to give us as our guide to duty and happiness; by which, as in a glass, we may survey ourselves, and know what manner of persons we are. James i, 23.

This discovers to ourselves what we are; pierces into the inmost recesses of the mind; strips off every disguise; lays open the inward part; makes a strict scrutiny into the very soul and spirit; and critically judges of the thoughts and intents of the heart. It shows with what exactness and care we are to search and try our spirits, examine ourselves, and watch our ways, and keep our hearts, in order to acquire this important self-science; which it often calls us to do. "Examine yourselves; prove your own selves; know you not yourselves?* Let a man examine himself." 1 Cor. xi, 28. Our Saviour upbraids his disciples

* Though the Greek word, 2 Cor. xiii, 5, signifies to approve as well as to prove, yet that our translators have hit upon the true sense of the word here, in rendering it prove yourselves, is apparent, not only from the word immediately preceding, which is of the same import, but because self-probation is always necessary to a right self-approbation.

" Every Christian ought to try himself, and may know himself if he be faithful in examining. The frequent exhortations of Scripture hereunto imply both these, viz., that the knowledge of ourselves is attainable, and that we should endeavour after it. Why should the apostle put them upon examining and proving themselves, unless it was possible to know themselves upon such trying and proving?"—*Bennet's Christian Oratory*, p. 568.

with their self-ignorance, in not knowing "what manner of spirits they were of," Luke ix, 55. And saith the apostle, "If a man (through self-ignorance) thinketh himself to be something when he is nothing, he deceiveth himself. But let every man prove his work, and then shall he have rejoicing in himself, and not in another." Gal. vi, 3, 4. Here we are commanded, instead of judging others, to judge ourselves; and to avoid the inexcusable rashness of condemning others for the very crimes we ourselves are guilty of, which a self-ignorant man is very apt to do; nay, to be more offended at a small blemish in another's character, than at a greater in his own; upon which folly, self-ignorance, and hypocrisy, our Saviour with just severity animadverts. Matt. vii, 3–5.

And what stress was laid upon this under the Old Testament dispensation appears sufficiently from those expressions: "Keep thy heart with all diligence," Prov. iv, 23. "Commune with your own heart," Psalm iv, 4. "Search me, O God, and know my heart; try me, and know my thoughts," Psalm cxxxix, 23. "Examine me, O Lord, and prove me; try my reins and my heart," Psalm xxvi, 2. "Let us search and try our ways," Lam. iii, 4. "Recollect, recollect yourselves, O nation not desired,"* Zeph. ii, 1. And all this is necessary to that self-acquaintance which is the only proper basis of solid peace.†

Were mankind but more generally convinced of the importance and necessity of this self-knowledge, and possessed with a due esteem for it; did they but know the true way to attain it; and under a proper sense of its excellence, and the fatal effects of self-ignorance, did they but make it their business and study every day to cultivate it, how soon should we find a happy alteration in the manners and tempers of men! But the evil is, men will not think; will not employ their thoughts, in good earnest, about the things which most of all deserve and demand them. By which unaccountable indolence, and aversion to self-reflection, they are led, blindfold and insensibly, into the most

The Hebrew verb properly signifies to glean, or to gather together scattered sticks or straws; as appears from all the places where the word is used in the Old Testament. Exod. v, 7, 12; Num. xv, 32; 1 Kings xvii, 10. Hence by an easy metaphor it signifies to recollect, or to gather the scattered thoughts together; and ought in this place to be so rendered.

† Clemens Alexandrinus says, that Moses by that phrase, so common in his writings, Take heed to thyself, (Exod. x, 28; xxxiv, 12; Deut. iv, 9,) means the same thing as the ancients did by their "Know thyself."

dangerous path of infidelity and wickedness as the Jews were heretofore; of whose amazing ingratitude and apostasy God himself assigns this single cause: "my people do not consider," Isa. i, 3.*

Self-knowledge is that acquaintance with ourselves which shows us what we are, and do; and ought to be, and do, in order to our living comfortably and usefully here, and happily hereafter. The means of it is self-examination; the end of it self-government, and self-enjoyment. It principally consists in the knowledge of our souls; which is attained by particular attention to their various powers, capacities, passions, inclinations, operations, state, happiness, and temper. For a man's soul is properly himself. Matt. xvi, 26, compared with Luke ix, 25. The body is but the house, the soul is the tenant that inhabits it; the body is the instrument, the soul the artist that directs it.†

* "There is nothing men are more deficient in than knowing their own characters. I know not how this science comes to be so much neglected. We spend a great deal of time in learning useless things, but take no pains in the study of ourselves; and in opening the folds and doubles of the heart." —*Reflections on Ridicule*, p. 61.

† "When you talk of a man, I would not have you tack flesh and blood to the notion, nor those limbs which are made out

This science, which is to be the subject of the ensuing Treatise, hath these three peculiar properties in it, which distinguish it from, and render it preferable to, all others: (1.) "It is equally attainable by all." It requires no strength of memory, no force of genius, no depth of penetration, as many other sciences do, to come at a tolerable acquaintance with them; which therefore renders them inaccessible by the greatest part of mankind. Nor is it placed out of their reach, through a want of opportunity, and proper assistance and direction how to acquire it, as many other parts of learning are. Every one of a common capacity hath the opportunity and ability to acquire it, if he will but recollect his rambling thoughts, turn them in upon himself, watch the motions of his heart, and compare them with his rule. (2.) "It is of equal importance to all, and of the highest importance to every one."* Other sciences are suited to the various conditions of life. Some more necessary to some, others to others. But

of it; these are but tools for the soul to work with; and no more a part of a man, than an axe or a plain is a piece of a carpenter. It is true, nature hath glued them together, and they grow as it were to the soul, and there is all the difference."—*Collier.*

* "'Tis virtue only makes our bliss below,
And all our knowledge is OURSELVES TO KNOW."—*Pope.*

this equally concerns every one that hath an immortal soul, whose final happiness he desires and seeks. (3.) "Other knowledge is very apt to make a man vain; this always keeps him humble." Nay, it is always for want of this knowledge that men are vain of that they have. "Knowledge puffeth up," 1 Cor. viii, 1. A small degree of knowledge often hath this effect on weak minds. And the reason why greater attainments in it have not so generally the same effect, is, because they open and enlarge the views of the mind so far, as to let into it, at the same time, a good degree of self-knowledge: for the more true knowledge a man hath, the more sensible he is of the want of it, which keeps him humble.

And now, reader, whoever thou art, whatever be thy character, station, or distinction in life, if thou art afraid to look into thine heart, and hast no inclination to self-acquaintance, read no further, lay aside this book; for thou wilt find nothing here that will flatter thy self-esteem, but, perhaps, something that may abate it. But, if thou art desirous to cultivate this important kind of knowledge, and to live no longer a stranger to thyself, proceed; and keep thy eye open to thine own image, with whatever unexpected deformity it may present itself to thee;

and patiently attend, while, by divine assistance, I endeavour to lay open thine own heart to thee, and lead thee to the true knowledge of thyself, in the following chapters.

CHAPTER II.

The several branches of self-knowledge. We must know what sort of creatures we are, and what we shall be.

THAT we may have a more distinct and orderly view of this subject, I shall here consider the several branches of self-knowledge; or some of the chief particulars wherein it consists: whereby perhaps it will appear to be a more copious and comprehensive science than we imagine. And,

(1.) To know ourselves, is "to know and seriously consider what sort of creatures we are, and what we shall be."

1. "What we are."

Man is a complex being, τριμερης υποστασις, a *tripartite person*, or a compound creature, made up of three distinct parts, *viz.*, the *body*, which is the earthy or mortal part of him; the *soul*, which is the animal or sensitive part; and the *spirit*, or *mind*, which is the rational and immortal part. Each of these three parts has its respective office assigned it; and a man then acts becoming himself, when he keeps them duly employed in their proper functions, and preserves their natural subordination. But it is not enough to know this merely as a point of speculation; we must pursue and revolve the thought, and urge the consideration to all the purposes of a practical self-knowledge.

We are not all body, nor mere animal creatures. We have a more noble nature than the inanimate or brutal part of the creation. We can not only move and act freely, but we observe in ourselves a capacity of reflection, study, and forecast; and various mental operations, of which irrational animals discover no symptoms. Our souls, therefore, must be of a more excellent nature than theirs; and from the power of thought with which they are endowed, they are proved to be immaterial substances, and consequently, in their own nature, capable of immortality. And that they are actually immortal, or will never die, the sacred Scriptures do abundantly testify. Let us then hereupon seriously recollect ourselves in the following soliloquy.

"O my soul, look back but a few years, and

thou wast nothing! And how didst thou spring out of that nothing? Thou couldst not make thyself. That is quite impossible. Most certain it is, that the same almighty, self-existent, and eternal Power, which made the world, made thee also out of nothing, called thee into being when thou wast not, gave thee those reasoning and reflecting faculties which thou art now employing in searching out the end and happiness of thy nature. It was he, O my soul, that made thee intelligent and immortal. It was he that placed thee in this body, as in a prison; where thy capacities are cramped, thy desires debased, and thy liberty lost. It was he that sent thee into this world, which, by all circumstances, appears to be a state of short discipline and trial. And wherefore did he place thee here, when he might have made thee a more free, unconfined, and happy spirit? But check that thought; it looks like too presumptuous a curiosity. A more needful and important inquiry is, What did he place thee here for? And what doth he expect from thee, while thou art here? What part hath he allotted me to act on the stage of human life; where he, angels, and men, are spectators of my behaviour? The part he hath given me to act here is, doubtless, a very important one; because it is for eternity.* And what is it but to live up to the dignity of my rational and intellectual nature, and as becomes a creature born for immortality?

"And tell me, O my soul, (for, as I am now about to cultivate a better acquaintance with thee, to whom I have been too long a stranger, I must try thee, and put many a close question to thee,) tell me, I say, while thou confinest thy desires to sensual gratifications, wherein dost thou differ from the beasts that perish? Captivated by bodily appetites, dost thou not put thyself upon a level with the lower class of beings, which were made to serve thee; offer an indignity to thyself, and despise the work of thy Maker's hands? O remember thy heavenly extract; remember thou art a spirit! Check, then, the solicitations of the flesh; and dare to do nothing that may diminish thy native excellence, dishonour thy high original, or degrade thy noble nature. But let me still urge it. Consider, (I say,) O my soul, that thou art an immortal spirit. Thy body dies; but thou, *thou*

* It is said when Virgil was asked by his friend, why he studied so much accuracy in the plan of his poem, the propriety of his characters, and the purity of his diction, he replied, "I am writing for eternity." What more weighty consideration to justify and enforce the utmost vigilance and circumspection of life than this, "I am living for eternity."

must live for ever, and thy eternity must take its tincture from the manner of thy behaviour, and the habits thou contractest, during this thy short copartnership with flesh and blood. O! do nothing now but what thou mayest with pleasure look back upon a million of ages hence. For know, O my soul, that thy self-consciousness and reflecting faculties will not leave thee with thy body; but will follow thee after death, and be the instrument of unspeakable pleasure or torment to thee in that separate state of existence."

(2.) In order to a full acquaintance with ourselves, we must endeavour to know not only what we are, but what we shall be.

And O! what different creatures shall we soon be from what we now are! Let us look forward, then, and frequently glance our thoughts toward death; though they cannot penetrate the darkness of that passage, or reach the state behind it. That lies veiled from the eyes of our mind: and the great God hath not thought fit to throw so much light upon it, as to satisfy the anxious and inquisitive desires the soul hath to know it. However, let us make the best use we can of that little light which Scripture and reason have let in upon this dark and important subject.

"Compose thy thoughts, O my soul, and imagine how it will fare with thee when thou goest, a naked, unembodied spirit, into a world, an unknown world of spirits, with all thy self-consciousness about thee, where no material object shall strike thine eye, and where thy dear partner and companion, the body, cannot come nigh thee; but where, without it, thou wilt be sensible of the most noble satisfactions, or the most exquisite pains. Embarked in death, thy passage will be dark; and the shore, on which it will land thee, altogether strange and unknown. 'It doth not yet appear what we shall be.'"*

* "Thou must expire, my soul, ordain'd to range
Through unexperienced scenes, and myst'ries strange;
Dark the event, and dismal the exchange.
But, when compell'd to leave this house of clay,
And to an unknown somewhere wing thy way:
When time shall be eternity, and thou
Shalt be thou know'st not what, nor where, nor how,
Trembling and pale, what wilt thou see or do?
Amazing state! No wonder that we dread
The thoughts of death, or faces of the dead.
His black retinue sorely strikes our mind;
Sickness and pain before, and darkness all behind.
Some courteous ghost, the secret then reveal;
Teach us what you have felt, and we must feel.
You warn us of approaching death, and why
Will you not teach us what it is to die?
But having shot the gulf, you love to view

That revelation which God hath pleased to make of his will to mankind was designed rather to fit us for the future happiness, and direct our way to it, than open to us the particular glories of it, or distinctly show us what it is. This it hath left still very much a mystery; to check our too curious inquiries into the nature of it, and to bend our thoughts more intently to that which more concerns us, viz., an habitual preparation for it. And what that is, we cannot be ignorant, if we believe either our Bible or our reason. For both these assure us, that "that which makes us like to God, is the only thing that can fit us for the enjoyment of him." Here, then, let us hold. Let our great concern be, to be "holy as he is holy." And then, and then only, are we sure to enjoy him, "in whose light we shall see light." And, be the future state of existence what it will, we shall some way be happy there, and much more

---

Succeeding spirits plunged along like you;
Nor lend a friendly hand to guide them through.
When dire disease shall cut or age untie
The knot of life, and suffer us to die:
When, after some delay, some trembling strife,
The soul stands quiv'ring on the ridge of life;
With fear and hope she throbs, then curious tries
Some strange hereafter, and some hidden skies."

NORRIS.

happy than we can now conceive; though, in what particular manner we know not, because God hath not revealed it.

CHAPTER III.

The several relations in which we stand to God, to Christ, and our fellow-creatures.

II. "SELF-KNOWLEDGE requires us to be well acquainted with the various relations in which we stand to other beings, and the several duties that result from those relations." And,

(1.) "Our first and principal concern is to consider the relation we stand in to Him who gave us our being."

We are the creatures of his hand, and the objects of his care. His power upholds the being his goodness gave us; his bounty accommodates us with the blessings of this life; and his grace provides for us the happiness of a better. Nor are we merely his creatures, but his rational and intelligent creatures. It is the dignity of our natures, that we are capable of knowing and enjoying him that made us. And, as the rational creatures of God, there are two relations especially that we stand in to him;

the frequent consideration of which is absolutely necessary to a right, self-knowledge. For, as our Creator, he is our King and Father: and, as his creatures, we are the subjects of his kingdom, and the children of his family.

1. "We are the subjects of his kingdom." And, as such, we are bound,

(1.) To yield a faithful obedience to the laws of his kingdom. And the advantages by which these come to be recommended to us above all human laws, are many. They are calculated for the private interest of every one, as well as that of the public; and are designed to promote our present, as well as our future happiness. They are plainly and explicitly published; easily understood; and in fair and legible characters writ in every man's heart, and the wisdom, reason, and necessity of them are readily discerned. They are urged with the most mighty motives that can possibly affect the human heart. And, if any of them are difficult, the most effectual grace is freely offered to encourage and assist our obedience; advantages which no human laws have to enforce the observance of them. (2.) As his subjects, we must readily pay the homage due to his sovereignty. And this is no less than the homage of the heart; humbly acknowledging, that we hold every thing of him, and have every thing from him. Earthly princes are forced to be content with verbal acknowledgments, or mere formal homage ; for they can command nothing but what is external : but God, who knows and looks at the hearts of all his creatures, will accept of nothing but what comes from thence. He demands the adoration of our whole souls, which is most justly due to him, who formed them, and gave them the very capacities to know and adore him. (3.) As faithful subjects, we must cheerfully pay him the tribute he requires of us. This is not like the tribute which earthly kings exact; who as much depend upon their subjects for the support of their power, as their subjects do upon them for the protection of their property. But the tribute God requires of us, is a tribute of praise and honour; which he stands in no need of from us. For his power is independent, and his glory immutable; and he is infinitely able, of himself, to support the dignity of his universal government. But it is the most natural duty we owe him, as creatures. For, to praise him, is only to show forth his praise; to glorify him, to celebrate his glory; and to honour him, is to render him and his ways honourable in the eyes and esteem of others. And, as this is the most natural duty that creatures owe to their Creator, so, it is a tribute he requires of every one of them, in proportion to their respective talents and abilities to pay it. (4.) As dutiful subjects, we must contentedly and quietly submit to the methods and administrations of his government, however dark, involved, or intricate. All governments have their *arcana imperii*, or secrets of state, which common subjects cannot penetrate. And therefore, they cannot competently judge of the wisdom or rectitude of certain public measures; because they are ignorant either of the springs of them, or the ends of them, or the expediency of the means, arising from the particular situation of things in the present juncture. And how much truer is this with relation to God's government of the world, whose wisdom is far above our reach, and "whose ways are not as ours?" Whatever, then, may be the present aspect and appearance of things, as dutiful subjects, we are bound to acquiesce; to ascribe wisdom and "righteousness to our Maker," in confidence that the King and "Judge of all the earth will do right." Again, (5.) As good subjects of God's kingdom, we are bound to pay a due regard and reverence to his ministers: especially if they discover an uncorrupted fidelity to his cause, and a pure, unaffected zeal for his honour; if they do not seek their own interest more than that of their divine Master. The ministers of earthly princes too often do this; and it would be happy if all the ministers and ambassadors of the heavenly King were entirely clear of the imputation. It is no uncommon thing for the honour of an earthly monarch to be wounded through the sides of his ministers. The defamation and slander that are directly thrown at them, are obliquely intended against him: and as such they are taken. So, to attempt to make the ministers of the gospel, in general, the objects of derision, as some do, plainly shows a mind very dissolute and disaffected to God, and religion itself; and is to act a part very unbecoming the dutiful subjects of his kingdom. (Lastly.) As good subjects, we are to do all we can to promote the interest of his kingdom; by defending the wisdom of his administrations, and endeavouring to reconcile others thereunto, under all the darkness and difficulties that may appear in them, in opposition to the profane censures of the prosperous wicked, and the doubts and dismays of the afflicted righteous. This is to act in character, as loyal subjects of the King of heaven. And whoever forgets this part of his character, or acts contrary to it, shows a great degree of self-ignorance.

But, (2.) As the creatures of God, we are not only the subjects of his kingdom, but the children of his family. And to this relation, and the obligations of it, must we carefully attend, if we would attain the true knowledge of ourselves. We are his children by creation; in which respect he is truly our Father. Isa. lxiv, 8: "But now, O Lord, thou art our Father: we are the clay, and thou our potter; and we all are the work of thy hand." And in a more special sense we are his children by adoption. Gal. iii, 26: "For ye are all the children of God by faith in Christ Jesus." And, therefore, (1.) We are under the highest obligations to love him as our Father. The love of children to parents is founded on gratitude, for benefits received, which can never be requited; and ought in reason to be proportioned to those benefits; especially if they flow from a conscientiousness of duty in the parent. And what duty more natural than to love our benefactors? What love and gratitude then is due to Him from whom we have received the greatest benefit, even that of our being; and every thing that contributes to the comfort of it? (2.) As his children, we must honour him; that is, must speak honourably of him, and for him; and carefully avoid every thing that may tend to dishonour his holy name and ways. Mal. i, 6: "A son honoureth his father: if then I be a father, where is mine honour?" (3.) As our Father, we are to apply to him for what we want. Whither should children go but to their father for protection, help, and relief, in every danger, difficulty, and distress? And, (4.) We must trust his power, and wisdom, and paternal goodness, to provide for us, take care of us, and do for us that which is best. And what that is he knows best. To be anxiously fearful what will become of us, and discontented and perplexed under the apprehension of future evils, while we are in the hands, and under the care of our Father who is in heaven, is not to act like children. Earthly parents cannot avert from their children all the calamities they fear, because their wisdom and power are limited; but our all-wise and almighty Father in heaven can. They may possibly want love and tenderness for their offspring; but our heavenly Father cannot for his. Isa. xlix, 15. (5.) As children, we must quietly acquiesce in his disposals, and not expect to see into the wisdom of all his will. It would be indecent and undutiful in a child to dispute his parents' authority, or question their wisdom, or neglect their orders, every time he could not discern the reason and design of them. Much more unreasonable and unbecoming is such behaviour toward God, "who giveth not account of any of his matters; whose judgments are unsearchable, and whose ways are past finding out." Job xxxiii, 13; Rom. xi, 33. (Lastly.) As children, we must patiently submit to his discipline and correction. Earthly parents may sometimes punish their children through passion or caprice; but our heavenly Father always corrects his for their profit, (Heb. xii, 10,) and only if need be, (1 Peter i, 6,) and never so much as their iniquities deserve. Ezra ix, 13. Under his fatherly rebukes let us ever be humble and submissive. Such now is the true filial disposition. Such a temper and such a behaviour should we show toward God, if we would act in character as his children.

These then are the two special relations, which, as creatures, we stand in to God. And not to act toward him in the manner before-mentioned, is to show that we are ignorant of, or have not yet duly considered, our obligations to him as his subjects and his children; or that we are as yet ignorant both of God and ourselves. Thus we see how directly the knowledge of ourselves leads us to the knowledge of God. So true is the observation of a late pious and very worthy divine, that "he who is a stranger to himself, is a stranger to God, and to every thing that may denominate him wise and happy."

But, (2.) In order to know ourselves there is another important relation we should often think of, and that is, that in which we stand to Jesus Christ, our Redeemer.

The former was common to us as men: this is peculiar to us as Christians; and opens to us a new scene of duties and obligations, which a man can never forget that does not grossly forget himself. For, as Christians we are the disciples, the followers, and the servants of Christ, redeemed by him.

And, 1. As the disciples of Christ, we are to learn of him: to take our religious sentiments only from his gospel, in opposition to all the authoritative dictates of men, who are weak and fallible as ourselves. "Call no man master on earth." While some affect to distinguish themselves by party names, as the Corinthians formerly did, (for which the apostle blames them,) one saying, "I am of Paul;" another, "I am of Apollos;" another, "I am of Cephas," (1 Cor. i, 12,) let us remember, that we are the disciples of Christ, and in this sense, make mention of his name only. It is really injurious to it, to seek to distinguish ourselves by any other.

There is more carnality in such party distinctions, denominations, and attachments, than many good souls are aware of; though not more than the apostle Paul (who was unwillingly placed at the head of one himself) hath apprized them of. 1 Cor. iii, 4. We are of Christ: our concern is, to honour that superior denomination, by living up to it; and to adhere inflexibly to his gospel, as the *only* rule of our faith, the guide of our life, and the foundation of our hope; whatever contempt or abuse we may suffer, either from the profane or bigoted part of mankind, for so doing. (2.) As Christians, we are followers of Christ; and therefore bound to imitate him, and copy after that most excellent pattern he hath set us, "who hath left us an example, that we should follow his steps," 1 Peter ii, 21: to see that the same holy temper "be in us which was in him;" and to discover it in the same manner he did, and upon like occasions. To this he calls us. Matt. xi, 29. And no man is any further a Christian, than as he is a follower of Christ; aiming at a more perfect conformity to that most perfect example which he hath set us of universal goodness. (3.) As Christians, we are the servants of Christ; and the various duties which servants owe to their masters in any degree, those we owe to him in the highest degree ; who expects we should behave ourselves in his service with that fidelity and zeal, and steady regard to his honour and interest, at all times, which we are bound to by virtue of this relation, and which his unmerited and unlimited goodness and love lay us under infinite obligations to. (Lastly.) We are, moreover, his redeemed servants ; and, as such, are under the strongest motives to love and trust him.

This deserves to be more particularly considered, because it opens to us another view of the human nature in which we should often survey ourselves, if we desire to know ourselves ; and that is, as depraved or degenerate beings. The inward contest we so sensibly feel, at some seasons especially, between a good and a bad principle, (called, in Scripture language, the flesh and the spirit,) of which some of the wisest heathens seemed not to be ignorant ; this, I say, is demonstration, that some way or other the human nature has contracted an ill bias, (and how that came about, the sacred Scriptures have sufficiently informed us,) and that it is not what it was when it came originally out of the hands of its Maker ; so that the words which St. Paul spake, with reference to the Jews in particular, are justly applicable to the state of mankind in general, "There is none righteous, no, not one; they are all gone out of the way, they are together become unprofitable, there is none that doth good, no, not one."

This is a very mortifying thought, but an undeniable truth, and one of the first principles of that science we are treating of; and very necessary to be attended to, if we would be sensible of the duty and obligations we owe to Christ, as the great Redeemer, in which character he appears for the relief and recovery of mankind under this their universal depravity.

The two miserable effects of the human apostacy are, 1. That perverse dispositions grow up in our minds from early infancy, that soon settle into vicious habits, which render us weak, and unwilling to obey the dictates of conscience and reason, and is commonly called the dominion of sin. And, 2. At the same time we are subject to the displeasure of God, and the penalty of his law; which is commonly called the condemnation of sin. Now, in both these respects did Christ, "the Lamb of God, come to take away the sin of the world;" that is, to take away the reigning power of it by the operation of his grace; and the condemning power of it, by the atonement of his blood; to sanctify us by his Spirit and justify us by his death. By the former he reconciles us to God, and, by the latter, he reconciles God to us; and is, at once, our righteousness and strength. He died to purchase for us the happiness we had forfeited, and sends his grace and Spirit to fit us for that happiness he hath thus purchased. So complete is his redemption! so suitably adapted is the remedy he hath provided to the malady we had contracted! "O blessed Redeemer of wretched ruined creatures, how unspeakable are the obligations I owe thee! But, ah! how insensible am I of those obligations! The saddest symptom of degeneracy I find in my nature, is that base ingratitude of heart, which renders me so unaffected with thine astonishing compassions. Till I know thee, I cannot know myself; and when I survey myself, may I ever think of thee! may the daily consciousness of my weakness and guilt lead my thoughts to thee; and may every thought of thee kindle in my heart the most ardent glow of gratitude to thee, O thou divine, compassionate Friend, Lover, and Redeemer of mankind."

Whoever, then, he be, that calls himself a Christian, that is, who professes to take the gospel of Christ for a divine revelation, and the only rule of his faith and practice, but, at the same time, pays a greater regard to the dictates of men than to the doctrine of Christ; who loses sight of that great example of Christ which should animate his Christian walk, is unconcerned about his service, honour, and interest, and excludes the consideration of his merits and atonement from his hope and happiness: he forgets that he is a Christian; he does not consider in what relation he stands to Christ, (which is one great part of his character,) and consequently discovers a great degree of self-ignorance.

(3.) Self-knowledge, moreover, implies a due attention to the several relations in which we stand to our fellow-creatures, and the obligations that result from thence.

If we know ourselves, we shall remember the condescension, benignity, and love, that is due to inferiors; the affability, friendship, and kindness, we ought to show to equals; the regard, deference, and honour, we owe to superiors; and the candor, integrity, and benevolence, we owe to all.

The particular duties requisite in these relations are too numerous to be here mentioned. Let it suffice to say, that, if a man doth not well consider the several relations of life in which he stands to others, and does not take care to preserve the decorum and propriety of those relations, he may justly be charged with self-ignorance.

And this is so evident in itself, and so generally allowed, that nothing is more common than to say, when a person does not behave with due decency toward his superiors, such a one does not understand himself. But why may not this with equal justice be said of those who act in an ill manner toward their inferiors? The expression, I know, is not so often thus applied; but I see no reason why it should not; since one is as common and as plain an instance of self-ignorance as the other. Nay, of the two, perhaps, men in general are more apt to be defective in their duty and behaviour toward those beneath them, than they are toward those that are above them; and the reason seems to be, because an apprehension of the displeasure of their superiors, and the detrimental consequences which may accrue from thence, may be a check upon them, and engage them to pay the just regards which they expect: but there being no such check to restrain them from violating the duties they owe to inferiors, (from whose displeasure they have little to fear,) they are more ready, under certain temptations, to treat them in an unbecoming manner. And as wisdom and self-knowledge will direct a man to be particularly careful, lest he neglect those duties he is most apt to forget; so, as to the duties he owes to inferiors, in which he is most in danger of transgressing, he ought more strongly to urge upon himself the indispensable obligations of religion and conscience. And if he does not, but suffers himself, through the violence of ungoverned passion, to be transported into the excesses of rigour, tyranny, and oppression, toward those whom God and nature have put into his power, it is certain he does not know himself, is not acquainted with his own particular weakness, is ignorant of the duty of his relation, and, whatever he may think of himself, hath not the true spirit of government, because he wants the art of self-government. For he that is unable to govern himself, can never be fit to govern others.

Would we know ourselves, then, we must consider ourselves as creatures, as Christians, and as men; and remember the obligations which, as such, we are under to God, to Christ, and our fellow-men, in the several relations in which we stand to them, in order to maintain the propriety, and fulfil the duties of those relations.

CHAPTER IV.

We must duly consider the rank and station of life in which Providence hath placed us, and what it is that becomes and adorns it.

III. A MAN, "that knows himself, will deliberately consider and attend to the particular rank and station in life in which Providence hath placed him; and what is the duty and decorum of that station; what part is given him to act; what character to maintain; and with what decency and propriety he acts that part, or maintains that character."

For a man to assume a character, or aim at a part, that does not belong to him, is affectation. And whence is it, that affectation of any kind appears so ridiculous, and exposes men to universal and just contempt, but because it is a certain indication of self-ignorance? Whence is it, that many seem so willing to be thought something when they are nothing, and seek to excel in those things in which they cannot, while they neglect those things in which they might excel? Whence is it, that they counteract the intention of nature and Providence, that when this intended them one thing they would fain be another? Whence, I say, but from an ignorance of themselves, the rank of life they are in, and the part and character which properly belong to them?

It is a just observation, and an excellent document of a moral heathen, that human life is a "drama, and mankind the actors, who have their several parts assigned them by the master of the theatre, who stands behind the scenes, and observes in what manner every one acts. Some have a short part allotted them, and some a long one; some a low, and some a high one. It is not he that acts the highest or most shining part on the stage, that comes off with the greatest applause; but he that acts his part best, whatever it be. To take care then to act our respective parts in life well, is ours: but to choose what part in life we shall act, is not ours, but God's."* But a man can never act his part well, if he does not attend to it; does

* Life is a stage-play; it matters not how long we act, so we act well, *Sen. Non est bonum, vivere, sed bene vivere.* It is not life, but living well, that is the blessing. Something similar to this is the epigram by Dr. Doddridge, on *dum vivimus vivamus*, which he assumed as his motto:—

"Live while you live, the epicure would say,
And seize the pleasures of the present day:
Live while you live, the sacred preacher cries,
And give to God each moment as it flies:
Lord! in my views let both united be:
I live in pleasure when I live to thee."

not know what becomes it; much less, if he affect to act another, which does not belong to him. It is always self-ignorance that leads a man to act out of character.

Is it a mean and low station in life thou art in? Know then, that Providence calls thee to the exercise of industry, contentment, submission, patience, hope, and humble dependance on him, and a respectful deference to thy superiors. In this way thou mayest shine through thy obscurity, and render thyself amiable in the sight of God and man. And not only so, but find more satisfaction, safety, and self-enjoyment, than they who move in a higher sphere, from whence they are in danger of falling.

But hath Providence called thee to act in a more public character, and for a more extensive benefit to the world? Thy first care, then, ought to be, that thy example, as far as its influence reaches, may be an encouragement to the practice of universal virtue. And next, to shine in those virtues especially which best adorn thy station; as, benevolence, charity, wisdom, moderation, firmness, and inviolable integrity: with an undismayed fortitude to press through all opposition in accomplishing those ends which thou hast a prospect and probability of attaining, for the apparent good of mankind.

And as self-acquaintance will teach us what part in life we ought to act, so the knowledge of that will show us whom we ought to imitate, and wherein. We are not to take example of conduct from those who have a very different part assigned them from ours ; unless in those things that are universally ornamental and exemplary. If we do, we shall but expose our affectation and weakness, and ourselves to contempt for acting out of character. For what is decent in one may be ridiculous in another. Nor must we blindly follow those who move in the same sphere, and sustain the same character with ourselves ; but only in those things that are befitting that character ; for it is not the person, but the character, we are to regard; and to imitate him no further than he keeps to that.

This caution especially concerns youth, who are apt to imitate their superiors very implicitly, especially such as excel in that part or profession which they themselves are aiming at: but for want of judgment to distinguish what is fit and decent, are apt to imitate their very foibles, which a partiality for their persons makes them deem as excellences ; and thereby they become doubly ridiculous, both by acting out of character themselves, and by a weak and servile imitation of others in the very things in which they do so too. To maintain a character then with decency, we must keep our eye only upon that which is proper to it.

In fine, as no man can excel in every thing, we must consider what part is allotted us to act, in the station in which Providence hath placed us, and keep to that, be it what it will, and seek to excel in that only.

CHAPTER V.

Every man should be well acquainted with his own talents and capacities; and in what manner they are to be exercised and improved to the greatest advantage.

IV. "A MAN cannot be said to know himself, till he is well acquainted with his proper talents and capacities; knows for what ends he received them; and how they may be most fitly applied and improved for those ends."

A wise and self-understanding man, instead of aiming at talents he hath not, will set about cultivating those he hath, as the way in which Providence points out his proper usefulness.

As, in order to the edification of the church, the Spirit of God at first conferred upon the ministers of it a great variety of spiritual gifts, 1 Cor. xii, 8–10 ; so for the good of the community, God is pleased now to confer upon men a great variety of natural talents. And "every one hath his proper gift of God, one after this manner, and another after that," 1 Cor. vii, 7. And every one is to take care "not to neglect, but to stir up the gift of God which is in him," 1 Tim. iv, 14 ; 2 Tim. i, 6. Because *it was given him to be improved*; and not only the abuse, but the neglect of it must be hereafter accounted for. Witness the doom of that unprofitable servant who laid up his single pound in a napkin ; and of him who went and hid his talent in the earth.

It is certainly a sign of great self-ignorance for a man to venture out of his depth, or attempt any thing he wants opportunity or capacity to accomplish. And therefore, a wise man will consider with himself, before he undertakes any thing of consequence, whether he hath abilities to carry him through it, and whether the issue of it is like to be for his credit ; lest he sink under the weight he lays upon himself, and incur the just censure of rashness, presumption, and folly. See Luke xiv, 28–32.*

* "He that takes up a burden that is too heavy for him, is in a fair way to break his back. In every business consider,

It is no uncommon thing for some, who excel in one thing, to imagine they may excel in every thing; and, not content with that share of merit which every one allows them, are still catching at that which does not belong to them. Why should a good orator affect to be a poet? Why must a celebrated divine set up for a politician? or a statesman affect the philosopher? or a mechanic the scholar? or a wise man labour to be thought a wit? This is a weakness that flows from self-ignorance, and is incident to the greatest men. Nature seldom forms a universal genius, but deals out her favours in the present state with a parsimonious hand. Many a man, by this foible, hath weakened a well-established reputation.*

first, what it is you are about; and then your own ability, whether it be sufficient to carry you through it."—*Epict.*

"Examine well, ye writers, weigh with care
What suits your genius, what your strength can bear;
For when a well-proportion'd theme you choose,
Nor words, nor method shall their aid refuse.
In this, or I mistake, consists the grace,
And force of method; to assign a place
For what with present judgment we should say,
And for some happier time the rest delay."

Francis's Horace.

* Cæcilius, a famous rhetorician of Sicily, who lived in the time of Augustus, and wrote a treatise on the sublime, (which is censured by Longinus in the beginning of his,) was a man of a hasty and enterprising spirit, and very apt to overshoot

CHAPTER VI.

We must be well acquainted with our inabilities, and those things in which we are naturally deficient, as well as those in which we excel.

V. "WE must, in order to a thorough self-acquaintance, not only consider our talents and proper abilities, but have an eye to our frailties and deficiencies, that we may know where our weakness as well as our strength lies." Otherwise, like Samson, we may run ourselves into infinite temptations and troubles.

Every man hath a weak side. Every wise man knows where it is, and will be sure to keep a double guard there.

There is some wisdom in concealing a weakness. This cannot be done, till it be first known; nor can it be known without a good degree of self-acquaintance.

It is strange to observe what pains some men are at to expose themselves; to signalize their own folly; and to set out to the most pub-

himself on all occasions; and particularly ventured far out of his depth in his comparison of Demosthenes and Cicero. Whereupon Plutarch made this sage and candid remark: "If," says he, "it were a thing obvious and easy for every man to know himself, possibly that saying, 'Know thyself,' had not passed for a divine oracle."

lic view those things which they ought to be ashamed to think should ever enter into their character. But so it is; some men seem to be ashamed of those things which should be their glory, while others "glory in their shame," Phil. iii, 19.

The greatest weakness in a man is to publish his weaknesses, and to appear fond to have them known. But vanity will often prompt a man to this, who, unacquainted with the measure of his capacities, attempts things out of his power, and beyond his reach, whereby he makes the world acquainted with two things to his disadvantage, which they were ignorant of before, namely, his deficiency and his self-ignorance, in appearing so blind to it.

It is ill-judged (though very common) to be less ashamed of a want of temper, than understanding. For it is no real dishonour or fault in a man to have but a small ability of mind, provided he hath not the vanity to set up for a genius, (which would be as ridiculous, as for a man of small strength and stature of body to set up for a champion,) because this is what he cannot help. But a man may, in a good measure, correct the fault of his natural temper, if he be well acquainted with it, and duly watchful over it. And, therefore, to betray a prevailing weakness of temper, or an ungoverned passion, diminishes a man's reputation much more than to discover a weakness of judgment or understanding. But what is most dishonourable of all is, for a man at once to discover a great genius and an ungoverned mind; because, that strength of reason and understanding he is master of, gives him a great advantage for the government of his passions; and, therefore, his suffering himself, notwithstanding, to be governed by them, shows, that he hath too much neglected or misapplied his natural talent, and willingly submitted to the tyranny of those lusts and passions, over which nature had furnished him with abilities to have secured an easy conquest.

A wise man hath his foibles, as well as a fool. But the difference between them is, that the foibles of the one are known to himself, and concealed from the world; the foibles of the other are known to the world, and concealed from himself. The wise man sees those frailties in himself which others cannot; but the fool is blind to those blemishes in his character which are conspicuous to every body else. Whence it appears, that self-knowledge is that which makes the main difference between a wise man and a fool, in the moral sense of that word.

CHAPTER VII.

Concerning the knowledge of our constitutional sins.

VI. "SELF-ACQUAINTANCE shows a man the particular sins he is most exposed and addicted to; and discovers not only what is ridiculous, but what is criminal, in his conduct and temper."

The outward actions of a man are generally the plainest index of his inward dispositions; and by the allowed sins of his life, you may know the reigning vices of his mind. Is he addicted to luxury and debauch? sensuality then appears to be his prevailing taste. Is he given to revenge and cruelty? choler and malice, then, reign in his heart. Is he confident, bold, and enterprising? ambition appears to be the secret spring. Is he sly and designing, given to intrigue and artifice? you may conclude, there is a natural subtlety of temper that prompts him to this. And this secret disposition is criminal, in proportion to the degree in which these outward actions, which spring from it, transgress the bounds of reason and virtue.

Every man hath something peculiar in the turn or cast of his mind, which distinguishes him as much as the particular constitution of his body. And both these, viz., his particular turn of mind, and particular constitution of body, incline and dispose him to some kind of sins much more than to others. And the same it is that renders the practice of certain virtues so much more easy to some than it is to others.*

Now, those sins which men generally are most strongly inclined to, and the temptations which they find they have least power to resist, are usually and properly called their constitutional

* Men, with regard to their bodies and bodily appetites, are pretty much alike; but with regard to their mental tastes and dispositions, they are often as different, as if they were quite of another species; governed by different views, entertained with different pleasures, animated with different hopes, and affected by different motives, and distinguished by different tempers and inclinations, as if they were not of the same kind. So that I am very ready to believe, that there is not a greater difference between an angel and some of the best and wisest of men, with regard to their temper and dispositions, than there is between some sort of men and others. And what inclines me to this sentiment is, considering the easy transition which nature always observes in passing from one order or kind of beings to another, together with the prodigious difference there appears to be between individuals of the human species, almost in every thing belonging to them. For there are some, "in whom one would think nature had placed every thing the wrong way;" depraved in their opinions, unintelligible in their reasoning, irregular in their actions, and vicious in every disposition. While in others we see almost every thing amiable and excellent that can adorn and exalt the human mind under the disadvantages of mortality.

sins; their peculiar frailties; and, in Scripture, their own iniquities, (Psa. xviii, 23,) and the sins which "do most easily beset them," Heb. xii, 1.

"As in the humours of the body, so in the vices of the mind, there is one predominant, which has an ascendant over us, and leads and governs us. It is in the body of sin what the heart is in the body of our nature; it begins to live first, and dies last; and, while it lives, it communicates life and spirit to the whole body of sin; and, when it dies, the body of sin expires with it. It is the sin to which our constitution leads, our circumstances betray, and custom enslaves us; the sin to which not our virtues only, but vices, too, lower their topsail, and submit; the sin which, when we would impose upon God and our conscience, we excuse and disguise with all imaginable artifice and sophistry: but, when we are sincere with both, we oppose first, and conquer last. It is, in a word, the sin which reigns and rules in the unregenerate, and too often alarms and disturbs (ah! that I could say no more) the regenerate."—*Lucas's Sermons*, vol. i, p. 151.

Some are more inclined to the sins of the flesh; sensuality, intemperance, uncleanness, sloth, self-indulgence, and excess in animal gratifications. Others more inclined to the sins of the spirit; pride, malice, covetousness, ambition, wrath, revenge, envy, &c. And I am persuaded there are few, but, upon a thorough search into themselves, may find that some one of these sins hath ordinarily a greater power over them than the rest. Others often observe it in them, if they themselves do not. And for a man not to know his predominant iniquity is great self-ignorance indeed, and a sign that he has all his life lived far from home ; because he is not acquainted with that in himself, which every one, who is but half an hour in his company, perhaps, may be able to inform him of. Hence proceeds that extreme weakness which some discover, in censuring others for the very same faults they are guilty of themselves, and, perhaps, in a much higher degree ; on which the apostle Paul animadverts, Rom. ii, 1.

It must be owned, it is an irksome and disagreeable business for a man to turn his own accuser; to search after his own faults, and keep his eye upon that which it gives him shame and pain to see. It is like tearing open an old wound. But it is better to do this than to let it mortify. The wounds of the conscience, like those of the body, cannot be well cured till they are searched to the bottom ; and they cannot be searched without pain. A man that is engaged in the study of himself must be content to know the worst of himself.

Do not, therefore, shut your eyes against your darling sin, or be averse to find it out. Why should you study to conceal or excuse it, and fondly cherish that viper in your bosom? "Some men deal by their sins, as some ladies do by their persons. When their beauty is decayed, they seek to hide it from themselves by false glasses, and from others by paint. So, many seek to hide their sins from themselves by false glosses, and from others by excuses, or false colours."—*Baxter*. But the greatest cheat they put upon themselves. "They that cover their sins shall not prosper," Prov. xxviii, 13. It is dangerous self-flattery to give soft and smoothing names to sins, in order to disguise their nature. Rather lay your hand upon your heart, and thrust it into your bosom, though it come out (as Moses's did) leprous as snow. Exod. iv, 6.*

* "The knowledge of sin is the first step toward amendment: for he that does not know he hath offended, is not willing to be reproved. You must therefore find out yourself before you can amend yourself. Some glory in their vices. And do you imagine they have any thoughts about reforming who place their very vices in the room of virtues? Therefore reprove thyself: search thyself very narrowly. First

And to find out our most beloved sin, let us consider what are those worldly objects or amusements which give us the highest delight: this, it is probable, will lead us directly to some one of our darling iniquities, if it be a sin of commission; and what are those duties which we read or hear of, from the word of God, to which we find ourselves most disinclined: and this, in all likelihood, will help us to detect some of our peculiar sins of omission, which, without such previous examination, we may not be sensible of. And thus may we make a proficiency in one considerable branch of self-knowledge.*

turn accuser to thyself, then a judge, and then a suppliant. And dare for once to displease thyself."—*Seneca.*

* "It is a good argument of a reformed mind, that it sees those vices in itself which it was before ignorant of."—*Seneca.*

A man's predominant sin usually arises out of his predominant passion; which, therefore, he should diligently observe. The nature and force of which is beautifully described by a great master of English verse:—

"On different senses different objects strike.
Hence different passions more or less inflame,
As strong or weak, the organs of the frame;
And hence one master-passion in the breast,
Like Aaron's serpent, swallows up the rest.
Nature its mother, habit is its nurse;
Wit, spirit, faculties, but make it worse;

CHAPTER VIII.

The knowledge of our most dangerous temptations necessary to self-knowledge.

VII. "A MAN, that rightly knows himself, is acquainted with his peculiar temptations; and knows when, and in what circumstances, he is in the greatest danger of transgressing."

Reader, if ever you would know yourself, you must examine this point thoroughly. And, if you have never yet done it, make a pause when you have read this chapter, and do it now. Consider in what company you are most apt to lose the possession and government of yourself; on what occasions you are apt to be most vain and unguarded, most warm and precipitant. Flee that company, avoid those occasions, if you would keep your conscience clear. What is it that robs you most of your time and your temper? If you have a due regard to the improvement of the one, and the preservation

---

Reason itself but gives it edge and power,
As heaven's blest beam turns vinegar more sour.
Ah! if she lend not arms as well as rules,
What can she more than tell us we are fools?
Teach us to mourn our nature, not to mend,
A sharp accuser, but a helpless friend!"—*Pope.*

of the other, you will regret such a loss, and shun the occasions of it, as carefully as you would a road beset with robbers.

But especially must you attend to the occasions which most usually betray you into your favourite vices; and consider the spring from whence they arise, and the circumstances which most favour them. They arise, doubtless, from your natural temper, which strongly disposes and inclines you to them. That temper, then, or particular turn of desire, must be carefully watched over as a most dangerous quarter. And the opportunities and circumstances which favour those inclinations must be resolutely avoided, as the strongest temptations. For the way to subdue a criminal inclination is, first, to avoid the known occasions that excite it, and then to curb the first motions of it. And thus, having no opportunity of being indulged, it will, of itself, in time, lose its force, and fail of its wonted victory.

The surest way to conquer, is sometimes to decline a battle; to weary out the enemy by keeping him at bay. Fabius Maximus did not use this stratagem more successfully against Hannibal, than a Christian may against his peculiar vice, if he be but watchful of his advantages. It is dangerous to provoke an unequal enemy to the fight, or to run into such a situation where we cannot expect to escape without a disadvantageous encounter.

It is of unspeakable importance, in order to self-knowledge and self-government, to be acquainted with all the accesses and avenues to sin, and to observe which way it is that we are oftenest led to it; and to set reason and conscience to guard those passes, those usual inlets to vice, which, if a man once enters, he will find a retreat extremely difficult.

"Watchfulness, which is always necessary, is chiefly so when the first assaults are made; for then the enemy is most easily repulsed, if we never suffer him to get within us, but, upon the very first approach, draw up our forces, and fight him without the gate. And this will be more manifest, if we observe by what methods and degrees temptations grow upon us. The first thing that presents itself to the mind is a plain, single thought; this, straight, is improved into a strong imagination; that, again, enforced by a sensible delight; then follow evil motions; and, when these are once stirred, there wants nothing but the assent of the will, and then the work is finished. Now, the first steps of this are seldom thought worth our care, sometimes not taken notice of; so that the enemy is frequently got close up to us, and even within our trenches, before we observe him."—*Thomas à Kempis*, p. 22.

As men have their particular sins, which do most easily beset them, so they have their particular temptations, which do most easily overcome them. That may be a very great temptation to one, which is none at all to another. And if a man does not know what are his greatest temptations, he must have been a great stranger, indeed, to the business of self-employment.

As the subtle enemy of mankind takes care to draw men gradually into sin, so he usually draws them, by degrees, into temptation. As he disguises the sin, so he conceals the temptation to it; well knowing, that, were they but once sensible of their danger of sin, they would be ready to be upon their guard against it. Would we know ourselves thoroughly, then, we must get acquainted, not only with our most usual temptations, that we be not unawares drawn into sin, but with the previous steps, and preparatory circumstances, which make way for those temptations, that we be not drawn unawares into the occasions of sin; for those things which lead us into temptations, are to be considered as temptations, as well as those which immediately lead us into sin. And a man that knows himself will be aware of his remote temptations, as well as the more immediate ones; for example, if he find the company of a passionate man is a temptation, (as Solomon tells us it is, Prov. xxii, 24, 25,) he will not only avoid it, but those occasions that may lead him into it. And the petition, in the Lord's prayer, makes it as much a man's duty to be upon his guard against temptation, as under it. Nor can a man pray from his heart, that God would not lead him into temptation, if he take no care himself to avoid it.

CHAPTER IX.

Self-knowledge discovers the secret prejudices of the heart.

VIII. Another important branch of self-knowledge is, for a man to be acquainted with his own prejudices, or those secret prepossessions of his heart, which, though so deep and latent that he may not be sensible of them, are often so strong and prevalent, as to give a mighty, but imperceptible, bias to the mind.

And in this the great art of self-knowledge consists, more than in any one thing again. It being, therefore, a matter of such mighty consequence, and, at the same time, a point to which men, in general, are too inattentive, it deserves a more particular discussion.

These prejudices of the human mind may be considered with regard to opinions, persons, and things.

(1.) With regard to opinions.

It is a common observation, but well expressed by a late celebrated writer, "that we set out in life with such poor beginnings of knowledge, and grow up under such remains of superstition and ignorance, such influences of company and fashion, such insinuations of pleasures, &c., that it is no wonder if men get habits of thinking only in one way; that these habits, in time, grow rigid and confirmed; and so their minds come to be overcast with thick prejudices, scarce penetrable by any ray of truth, or light of reason."—*See Religion of Nature delineated,* p. 129.

There is no man but is more fond of one particular set or scheme of opinions in philosophy, politics, and religion, than he is of another, if he hath employed his thoughts at all about them. The question we should examine, then, is, How come we by these attachments? whence are we so fond of those particular notions? did we come fairly by them? or, were they imposed upon us, and dictated to our easy belief, before we were able to judge of them? This is most likely. For the impressions we early receive, generally grow up with us, and are those we least care to part with. However, which way soever we came by them, they must be re-examined, and brought to the touch-stone of sound sense, solid reason, and plain Scripture. If they will not bear this, after hard rubbing, they must be discarded as no genuine principles of truth, but only counterfeits of it.

And, as reason and Scripture must discover our prejudices to us, so they only can help us to get rid of them. By these are we to rectify, and to these are we to conform all our opinions and sentiments in religion, as our only standard, exclusive of all other rules, light, or authority whatsoever.

And care must further be taken, that we do not make Scripture and reason bend and buckle to our notions, which will rather confirm our prejudices than cure them. For, whatever cannot evidently be made out, without the help of overstrained metaphors, and the arts of sophistry, is much to be suspected; which used to make Archbishop Tillotson say, *Non amo argutias in theologia*, "I do not love subtleties in divinity." But,

(2.) The human mind is very apt to be prejudiced, either for or against certain persons, as well as certain sentiments. And, as prejudice will lead a man to talk very unreasonably with regard to the latter, so it will lead him to act very unreasonably with regard to the former.

What is the reason, for instance, that we cannot help having a more hearty affection for some persons than others? Is it from a similarity of taste and temper? or something in their address, that flatters our vanity? or something in their humour, that hits our fancy? or something in their conversation, that improves our understanding? or a certain sweetness of disposition, and agreeableness of manner, that is naturally engaging? or from benefits received or expected from them? or from some eminent and distinguished excellence in them? or from none of these, but something else, we cannot tell what? Such sort of inquiries will show us, whether our esteem and affections be rightly placed, or flow from mere instinct, blind prejudice, or something worse.

And so, on the other hand, with regard to our disaffection toward any one, or the disgust we have taken against him; if we would know ourselves we must examine into the bottom of this, and see, not only what is the pretended, but true cause of it; whether it be a justifiable one, and our resentments duly proportioned to it. Is his manner of thinking, talking, and acting, quite different from mine, and therefore what I cannot approve? or have I received some real affront or injury from him? Be it so; my continued resentment against him, on either of these accounts, may be owing, notwithstanding, more to some unreasonable prejudice in me, than any real fault in him.

For, as to the former, his way of thinking, talking, and acting may possibly be juster than my own; which the mere force of custom and habit only makes me prefer to his. However, be his ever so wrong, he may not have had the same advantage of improving his understanding, address, and conduct, as I have had; and therefore his defects herein are more excusable. And he may have many other kind of excellences, which I have not. "But he is not only ignorant and unmannered, but insufferably vain, conceited, and overbearing at the same time." Why, that, perhaps, he cannot help; it is the fault of his nature. He is the object of pity, rather than resentment. And had I such a temper by nature, I should, perhaps, with all my self-improvement, find it a difficult thing to manage: and therefore, though I can never choose such a one for an agreeable companion, yet I ought not to harbour a dislike to him, but love, and pity, and pray for him, as a person under a great misfortune, and be thankful that I am not under the same. "But he is quite blind to this fault of his temper, and does not appear to be in the least sensible of it." Why, that is a greater misfortune still, and he ought to be the more pitied.

And as to the other pretended ground of prejudice, "He hath often offended and injured me," let me consider, 1. Whether any offence was really intended; whether I do not impute that to ill nature, which was only owing to ill manners; or that to design, which proceeded only from ignorance. Do I not take offence before it is given? If so, the fault is mine, and not his: and the resentment I have conceived against him, I ought to turn upon myself.* Again, 2. Did I not provoke him to it, when I knew his temper? The fault is still my own. I did, or might know, the pride, passion, or perverseness of his nature; why, then, did I

* "For every trifle scorn to take offence;
That always shows great pride, or little sense.
Good nature and good sense must always join;
To err is human, to forgive divine."—*Pope.*

exasperate him? A man that will needlessly rouse a lion, must not expect always to come off so favourably as the hero of La Mancha. But, 3. Suppose I were not the aggressor, yet, how came I into his company? who led me into the temptation? He hath acted according to his nature in what he hath done; but I have not acted according to my reason, in laying myself so open to him. I knew him; why did I not shun him, as I would any other dangerous animal, that does mischief by instinct? If I must needs put my finger into a wasps' nest, why should I blame them for stinging me? Or, 4. If I could not avoid his company, why did I not arm myself? Why did I venture, defenceless, into so much danger? Or, 5. Suppose he hath done me a real and undeserved injury, without my fault or provocation, yet, does not my present discontent greatly aggravate it? Does it not appear greater to me than it does to any body else? or than it will to me, after the present ferment is over? And, lastly, after all, must I never forgive? How shall I be able to repeat the Lord's prayer, or read our Saviour's comment upon it, (Matt. vi, 14, 15,) with an unforgiving temper? Do I not hope to be forgiven ten thousand talents? and cannot I forgive my fellow-servant thirty pence, when I know not but he hath repented, and God hath forgiven him, whose forgiveness I want infinitely more than my greatest enemy does mine.*

Such considerations are of great use to soften our prejudices against persons; and at once to discover the true spring, and prevent the bad effects of them. And happy would it be for a Christian, could he but call to mind, and apply to his relief, half the good things which that excellent heathen emperor and philosopher,

* A man despises me: what then? Did he know me more, he would perhaps despise me more. But I know myself better than he can know me; and therefore despise myself more. And though his contempt, in this instance, may be groundless, yet in others it would be but too well founded. I will therefore not only bear with, but forgive it.

It has been reckoned a wise and witty answer which one of the philosophers returned to his friend, who advised him to revenge an injury that had been done him: "What!" says he, "if an ass kicks me, must I needs kick him again?" And, perhaps, there is more wit than wisdom in that reply. It seems, indeed, to carry in it something of a true greatness of mind; but does it not at the same time discover a kind of haughty and contemptuous spirit? The truth is, as a judicious writer observes, "It is at best but a lame and misshapen charity; it has more of pride than goodness. We should learn of the holy Jesus, who was not only meek, but lowly. We should contemn the injury, and pity the weakness; but should not disdain or despise the persons of our enemies. Charity vaunteth not herself, is not puffed up, doth not behave itself unseemly."--See *Scougal's Duty of Loving our Enemies.*

Marcus Antoninus, could say upon this subject; some of which I have, for the benefit of the English reader, extracted, and thrown into the margin.*

(3.) The mind is apt to be prejudiced against

* "In the morning remember to say to thyself, This day, perhaps, I may meet with some impertinent, ungrateful, peevish, tricking, envious, churlish fellow. Now all these ill qualities proceed from an ignorance of good and evil. And since I am so happy as to understand the natural beauty of a good action, and the deformity of an ill one; and since the person that disobliges me is of near kin to me; and though not just of the same blood and family, yet of the same divine extract as to his mind; and, finally, since I am convinced that no one can do me a real injury, because he cannot force me to do a dishonest thing; for these reasons I cannot find in my heart to hate him, or so much as to be angry with him."—*Marc. Anton. Medit.*, b. 2, § 1.

"You are just taking leave of the world, and have you not yet learned to be friends with every body? And that to be an honest man, is the only way to be a wise one."—*Ibid.*, b. 4, § 37.

"To expect an impossibility is madness; now it is impossible for ill men not to do ill things."—*Ibid.*, b. 5, § 17.

"A man misbehaves himself toward me; what is that to me? Let him look to that, for the action is his, and he acts according to his own disposition. As for me, I am in the condition Providence would have me, and am doing what becomes me."—*Ibid.*, b. 4, § 25.

"It is the privilege of human nature above brutes to love those that offend us. In order to this consider, (1.) That the offending party is of kin to you. (2.) That he acts thus, because he knows no better. (3.) He may have no design to offend you. (4.) You will both of you quickly be in your graves. But above all, (5.) You have received no harm or in favour of certain things and actions, as well as certain sentiments and persons.

If, therefore, you find in yourself a secret

from him; for your mind or reason is the same as before."—*Ibid.*, b. 7, § 22.

"Think upon your last hour, and do not trouble yourself about other people's faults, but leave them there where they must be answered for."—*Ibid.*, b. 7, § 29.

"Do not return the temper of ill-natured people upon themselves, nor treat them as they do the rest of mankind."—*Ibid.*, b. 7, § 55.

"Though the gods are immortal, yet they not only patiently bear with a wicked world through so many ages, but what is more, liberally provide for it: and are you, who are just going off the stage, weary with bearing, though you are one of those unhappy mortals yourself?"—*Ibid.*, b. 7, § 70.

"Never disturb yourself; for men will do the same untoward actions over again, though you burst with spleen."—*Ibid.*, b. 8, § 4.

"Reform an injurious person if you can: if not, remember your patience was given you to bear with him; that the gods patiently bear with such men, and sometimes bestow upon them health, and fame, and fortune."—*Ibid.*, b. 9, § 11.

"When people treat you ill, and show their spite and slander you, enter into their little souls, go to the bottom of them, search their understandings; and you will soon see, that nothing they may think or say of you need give you one troublesome thought."—*Ibid.*, b. 9, § 27.

"That is the best thing for a man which God sends him; and that is the best time when he sends it."—*Ibid.*, b. 9, § 27.

"It is sometimes a hard matter to be certain, whether you have received ill usage or not; for men's actions oftentimes look worse than they are: and one must be thoroughly informed of a great many things, before he can rightly judge."—*Ibid.*, b. 11, § 18.

disinclination to any particular action or duty, and the mind begins to cast about for excuses and reasons to justify the neglect of it, consider the matter well; go to the bottom of that reluctance, and search out what it is that gives the mind this aversion to it; whether it be the thing or action itself, or some discouraging circumstances that may attend it, or some disagreeable consequences that may possibly flow from it, or your supposed unfitness for it at present. Why, all these things may be only imaginary. And to neglect a plain and positive duty, upon such considerations, shows that you are governed by appearances more than realities, by fancy more than reason, and by inclination more than conscience.

"Consider how much more you often suffer from your anger and grief, than those very things for which you are angry and grieved."—*Ibid.*, b. 11, § 18.

"When you fancy any one hath transgressed, say thus to yourself: 'How do I know it is a fault? But admit it is, it may be his conscience hath corrected him; and then he hath received his punishment from himself.'"—*Ibid.*, b. 12, § 16.

To these I shall add two more quotations, out of the sacred writings, of incomparably greater weight and dignity than any of the fore-mentioned. Prov. xix, 11: "The discretion of a man deferreth his anger: and it is his glory to pass over a transgression." Rom. xii, 20, 21: "If thine enemy hunger, feed him: if he thrst, give him drink: for in so doing, thou shalt heap coals of fire on his head. Be not overcome of evil, but overcome evil with good."

But let fancy muster up all the discouraging circumstances, and set them in the most formidable light, to bar your way to a supposed duty; for instance, "It is very difficult, I want capacity, at least I am so indisposed to it at present, that I shall make nothing of it; and then it will be attended with danger to my person, reputation, or peace; and the opposition I am like to meet with is great," &c. But, after all, is the call of Providence clear? is the thing a plain duty, such as reason, conscience, and Scripture, your office, character, or personal engagement, call upon you to discharge? If so, all the aforesaid objections are vain and delusive; and you have nothing to do but to summon your courage, and, in dependance on divine help, to set about the business immediately, and in good earnest, and in the best and wisest manner you can; and, you may depend upon it, you will find the greatest difficulty to lie only in the first attempt; these frightful appearances to be all visionary, the mere figments of fancy, turning lambs into lions, and molehills into mountains; and that nothing but sloth, folly, and self-indulgence, thus set your imagination on work, to deter you from a plain duty. Your heart would deceive you; but you have found out the cheat, and do not be imposed upon.*

Again, suppose the thing done; consider how it will look then. Take a view of it as past; and, whatever pains it may cost you, think whether it will not be abundantly recompensed by the inward peace and pleasure which arise from a consciousness of having acted right. It certainly will. And the difficulties you now dread will enhance your future satisfaction. But think again how you will bear the reflections of your own mind, if you wilfully neglect a plain and necessary duty; whether this will not occasion you much more trouble than all the pains you might be at in performing it. And a wise man will always determine himself by the end, or by such a retrospective view of things, considered as past.

Again, on the other hand, if you find a strong propension to any particular action, examine that with the like impartiality. Perhaps, it is what neither your reason nor conscience can fully approve; and yet every motive to it is strongly urged, and every objection against it

* "The wise and prudent conquer difficulties
By daring to attempt them. Sloth and folly
Shiver and shrink at sight of toil and danger,
And make th' impossibility they fear."—*Rowe.*

slighted. Sense and appetite grow importunate and clamorous, and want to lead, while reason remonstrates in vain. But turn not aside from that faithful and friendly monitor, while, with a low still voice, she addresses you in this soft but earnest language: "Hear me, I beseech you, but this one word more. The action is indeed out of character; what I shall never approve. The pleasure of it is a great deal overrated; you will certainly be disappointed. It is a false appearance that now deceives you. And what will you think of yourself when it is past, and you come to reflect seriously on the matter? Believe it, you will then wish you had taken me for your counsellor, instead of those enemies of mine, your lusts and passions, which have so often misled you, though, you know, I never did."

Such short recollections as these, and a little leisure to take a view of the nature and consequences of things or actions, before we reject or approve them, will prevent much false judgment and bad conduct, and, by degrees, wear off the prejudices which fancy has fixed in the mind, either for or against any particular action; teach us to distinguish between things and their appearances; strip them of those false colours that so often deceive us; correct the sallies of the imagination, and leave the reins in the hand of reason.

Before I dismiss this head, I must observe, that some of our strongest prejudices arise from an excessive self-esteem, or too great value for our own good sense and understanding. Philautus, in every thing, shows himself very well satisfied with his own wisdom, which makes him very impatient of contradiction, and gives him a distaste to all who shall presume to oppose their judgment to his in any thing. He had rather persevere in a mistake than retract it, lest his judgment should suffer, not considering that his ingenuity and good sense suffer much more by such obstinacy. The fulness of his self-sufficiency makes him blind to those imperfections which every one can see in him but himself. So that, however wise, sincere, and friendly, however gentle and seasonable your remonstrance may be, he takes it immediately to proceed from ill-nature or ignorance in you, but from no fault in him.

Seneca, I remember, tells us a remarkable story, which very well illustrates this matter. Writing to his friend Lucilius, "My wife," says he, "keeps Harpastes in her house still, who, you know, is a sort of family fool, and an incumbrance upon us. For my part, I am far from taking any pleasure in such prodigies. If I have a mind to divert myself with a fool, I have not far to go for one; I can laugh at myself. This silly girl, all on a sudden, lost her eye-sight; and (which, perhaps, may seem incredible, but it is very true) she does not know she is blind, but is every now and then desiring her governess to lead her abroad, saying, the house is dark. Now, what we laugh at in this poor creature, we may observe, happens to us all. No man knows that he is covetous or insatiable. Yet, with this difference, the blind seek somebody to lead them, but we are content to wander without a guide. But why do we thus deceive ourselves? The disease is not without us, but fixed deep within. And therefore is the cure so difficult, because we do not know that we are sick."*

* Sen. Epist. 51.

" The reflection calculated above all others to allay that temper [referred to in the former part of this chapter] which is ever finding out provocations, and which renders anger so impetuous, is, that we ourselves are, or shortly shall be suppliants for mercy and pardon at the judgment seat of God; casting ourselves on his compassion; crying out for mercy: imagine such a creature to talk of satisfaction and revenge; refusing to be entreated; disdaining to forgive; extreme to mark and to resent what is done amiss: imagine this, and you can hardly bring to yourself an instance of more impious and unnatural arrogance."—*Paley*, *Mor. Phil.*

CHAPTER X.

The necessity and means of knowing our natural tempers.

IX. "Another very important branch of self-knowledge is, the knowledge of those governing passions or dispositions of the mind which generally form what we call a man's natural temper."

The difference of natural tempers seems to be chiefly owing to the different degrees of influence the several passions have upon the mind: for example, if the passions are eager, and soon raised, we say, the man is of a warm temper; if more sluggish, and slowly raised, he is of a cool temper; according as anger, malice, or ambition, prevail, he is of a fierce, churlish, or haughty temper; the influence of the softer passions of love, pity, and benevolence, forms a sweet, sympathizing, and courteous temper; and where all the passions are duly poised, and the milder and pleasing ones prevail, they make what is commonly called, a quiet, good-natured man.

So that, it is the prevalence or predominance of any particular passion, which gives the turn or tincture to a man's temper, by which he is distinguished, and for which he is loved and esteemed, or shunned and despised, by others.

Now, what this is, those we converse with are soon sensible of. They presently see through us, and know the fault of our temper, and order their behaviour to us accordingly. If they are wise and well-mannered, they will avoid touching the string, which, they know, will jar and raise a discord within us. If they are our enemies, they will do it on purpose to set us on tormenting ourselves. And our friends we must suffer sometimes, with a gentle hand, to touch it, either by way of pleasant raillery, or faithful advice.

But a man must be greatly unacquainted with himself, if he is ignorant of his predominant passion, or distinguishing temper, when every one else observes it. And yet, how common is this piece of self-ignorance! The two apostles, Peter and John, discovered it in that very action wherein they meant to express nothing but a hearty zeal for their Master's honour; which made him tell them, that they knew not what manner of spirit they were of," Luke ix, 55; that is, that, instead of a principle of love and genuine zeal for Him, they were, at that time, governed by a spirit of pride, revenge, and cruelty. And that the apostle John should be liable to this censure, whose temper seemed to be all love and sweetness, is a memorable instance how difficult a thing it is for a man at all times to know his own spirit; and that that passion, which seems to have the least power over his mind, may, on some occasions, insensibly gain a criminal ascendant there.

And the necessity of a perfect knowledge of our reigning passions appears further from hence; because they not only give a tincture to the temper, but to the understanding also, and throw a strong bias on the judgment. They have much the same effect upon the eye of the mind, as some distempers have upon the eyes of the body; if they do not put it out, they weaken it, or throw false colours before it, and make it form a wrong judgment of things: and, in short, are the source of those fore-mentioned prejudices, which so often abuse the human understanding.

Whatever the different passions themselves that reign in the mind may be owing to; whether to the different texture of the bodily organs, or the different quality or motion of the animal spirits, or to the native turn and cast of the soul itself; yet certain it is, that men's different ways of thinking are much according to the predominance of their different passions, and especially with regard to religion. Thus, for example, we see melancholy people are apt to throw too much gloom upon their religion, and represent it in a very uninviting and unlovely view, as all austerity and mortification; while they, who are governed by the more gay and cheerful passions, are apt to run into the other extreme, and too much to mingle the pleasures of sense with those of religion; and are as much too lax as the other too severe. And so, by the prejudice or bias of their respective passions, or the force of their natural temper, are led into the mistake on both sides.

"So that, would a man know himself, he must study his natural temper, his constitutional inclinations and favourite passions; for, by these, a man's judgment is easily perverted, and a wrong bias hung upon his mind: these are the inlets of prejudice, the unguarded avenues of the mind, by which a thousand errors and secret faults find admission, without being observed or taken notice of."—*Spectator*, vol. vi, No. 899.

And, that we may more easily come at the knowledge of our predominant affections, let us consider what outward events do most impress and move us, and in what manner? What is it that usually creates the greatest pain or pleasure in the mind? As for pain, a stoic, indeed, may tell us, "that we must keep things at a distance; let nothing that is outward come within us; let externals be externals still." But the human make will scarce bear the rigour of that philosophy. Outward things, after all, will impress and affect us. And there is no harm in this, provided they do not get the possession of us, overset our reason, or lead us to act unbecoming a man or a Christian. And one advantage we may reap from hence is, the manner or degree in which outward things impress us, may lead us into a more perfect knowledge of ourselves, and discover to us our weak side, and the particular passions which have most power over us.

Our pleasures will likewise discover our reigning passions, and the true temper and disposition of the soul. If it be captivated by the pleasures of sin, it is a sign its prevailing taste is very vicious and corrupt; if with the pleasures of sense, very low and sordid; if imaginary pleasures, and the painted scenes of fancy and romance, do most entertain it, the soul hath then a trifling turn; if the pleasures of science, or intellectual improvements, are those it is most fond of, it has then a noble and refined taste; but, if the pleasures of religion and divine contemplation do, above all others, delight and entertain it, it has then its true and proper taste;

its temper is, as it should be, pure, divine, and heavenly, provided these pleasures spring from a true religious principle, free from that superstition, bigotry, and enthusiam, under which it is often disguised.

And thus, by carefully observing what it is that gives the mind the greatest pain and torment, or the greatest pleasure and entertainment, we come at the knowledge of its reigning passions, and prevailing temper and disposition.

"Include thyself, then, O my soul, within the compass of thine own heart; if it be not large, it is deep; and thou wilt there find exercise enough. Thou wilt never be able to sound it; it cannot be known but by Him who tries the thoughts and reins. But dive into this subject as deep as thou canst. Examine thyself; and this knowledge of that which passes within thee will be of more use to thee than the knowledge of all that passes in the world. Concern not thyself with the wars and quarrels of public or private persons. Take cognizance of those contests which are between thy flesh and thy spirit: between the law of thy members, and that of thy understanding. Appease those differences. Teach thy flesh to be in subjection. Replace reason on its throne; and give it piety for its counsellor. Tame thy passions, and bring them under bondage. Put thy little state in good order; govern wisely and holily those numerous people which are contained in so little a kingdom; that is to say, that multitude of affections, thoughts, opinions, and passions, which are in thine heart."—*Jurieu's Method of Christian Devotion*, part iii, chap. 3.

CHAPTER XI.

Concerning the secret springs of our actions.

X. "Another considerable branch of self-acquaintance is, the knowledge of the true motives and secret springs of our actions."

And this sometimes cannot, without much pains, be acquired. But, for want of it, we shall be in danger of passing a false judgment upon our actions, and of having a wrong opinion of several parts of our conduct.

It is not only very possible, but very common, for men to be ignorant of the chief inducements of their behaviour; and to imagine they act from one motive, while they are apparently governed by another. If we examine our views, and look into our hearts narrowly, we shall find that they more frequently deceive us in this respect than we are aware of, by persuading us, that we are governed by much better motives than we are. The honour of God, and the interest of religion, may be the open and avowed motive, while secular interest and secret vanity may be the hidden and true one. While we think we are serving God, we may be only sacrificing to mammon. We may, like Jehu, boast our zeal for the Lord, when we are only animated by the heat of our natural passions; may cover a censorious spirit under a cloak of piety; and giving admonitions to others, may be only giving vent to our spleen.

How many come to the place of public worship out of custom or curiosity, who would be thought to come thither only out of conscience? And while their external and professed view is to serve God, and gain good to their souls, their secret and inward motive is only to show themselves to advantage, or to avoid singularity, and prevent others making observations on their absence. Munificence and almsgiving may often proceed from a principle of pride and party spirit, when it may appear to be the effect of pure piety and charity; and seeming acts of friendship, from a motive of selfishness.

By thus disguising our motives, we may impose upon men, but, at the same time, we impose upon ourselves; and, while we are deceiving others, our own hearts deceive us. And, of all impostures, self-deception is the most dangerous, because least suspected.

Now, unless we examine this point narrowly, we shall never come to the bottom of it; and unless we come at the true spring and real motive of our actions, we shall never be able to form a right judgment of them; and they may appear very different in our own eye, and in the eye of the world, from what they do in the eye of God. "For the Lord seeth not as man seeth: for man looketh on the outward appearance, but the Lord looketh on the heart," 1 Sam. xvi, 7. And hence it is, that "that which is highly esteemed among men, is oftentimes abomination in the sight of God," Luke xvi, 15. "Every way of man is right in his own eyes; but the Lord pondereth the heart," Prov. xxi, 2.

CHAPTER XII.

Every one that knows himself, is, in a particular manner, sensible how far he is governed by a thirst for applause.

XI. "ANOTHER thing necessary to unfold a man's heart to himself, is to consider what is his appetite *for fame*, and by what means he seeks to *gratify* that particular passion."

This passion, in particular, having always so main a stroke, and oftentimes so unsuspected an influence on the most important parts of our conduct, a perfect acquaintance with it is a very material branch of self-knowledge, and therefore requires a distinct and particular consideration.

Emulation, like the other passions of the human mind, shows itself much more plainly, and works much more strongly, in some, than it does in others. It is, in itself, innocent, and was planted in our natures for very wise ends, and is capable of serving very excellent purposes, if kept under proper restrictions and regulations. But, without these, it degenerates into a mean and criminal ambition.

When a man finds something within him that pushes him on to excel in worthy deeds, or in actions truly good and virtuous, and pursues that design with a steady unaffected ardour, without reserve or falsehood, it is a true sign of a noble spirit: for that love of praise can never be criminal that excites and enables a man to do a great deal more good than he could do without it. And perhaps there never was a fine genius, or a noble spirit, that rose above the common level, and distinguished itself by high attainments in what was truly excellent, but was secretly, and perhaps insensibly, prompted by the impulse of this passion.

But, on the contrary, if a man's views centre only in the applause of others, whether it be deserved or not; if he pants after popularity and fame, not regarding how he comes by them; if his passion for praise urge him to stretch himself beyond the line of his capacity, and to attempt things to which he is unequal; to condescend to mean arts and low dissimulation, for the sake of a name; and in a sinister, indirect way, sue hard for a little incense, not caring from whom he receives it; it then degenerates into what is properly called vanity. And if it excites a man to wicked attempts, and makes him willing to sacrifice the esteem of all wise and good men, to the shouts of the giddy multitude; if his ambition overleaps the bounds of decency and truth, and breaks through obligations of honour and virtue; it is then not only vanity, but vice; a vice the most destructive to the peace and happiness of human society, and which, of all others, hath made the greatest havoc and devastation among men.

What an instance have we here of the wide difference between common opinion and truth! That a vice, so big with mischief and misery, should be mistaken for a virtue! and that they, who have been most infamous for it, should be crowned with laurels, even by those who have been ruined by it, and have those laurels perpetuated by the common consent of men through after ages! Seneca's judgment of Alexander is certainly more agreeable to truth than the common opinion; who called him "a public cut-throat, rather than a hero; and who, in seeking only to be a terror to mankind, arose to no greater an excellence than what belonged to the most hurtful and hateful animals on earth."*

Certain it is, that these false heroes are, of

* How different from this is the judgment of Plutarch in this matter? who, in his oration concerning the fortune and virtue of Alexander, exalts him into a true hero; and justifies all the waste he made of mankind under (the same colour with which the Spaniards excused their inhuman barbarities toward the poor Indians, viz.) a pretence of civilizing them. And in attributing all his success to his virtue, he talks more

all men, most ignorant of themselves, who seek their gain and glory from the destruction of their own species; and, by this wicked ambition, entail infamy and curses upon their name and family, instead of that immortal glory they pursued, and imagined they had attained. According to the prophet's words, "Wo to him who coveteth an evil covetousness to his house, that he may set his nest on high; that he may be delivered from the power of evil. Thou hast consulted shame to thine house, by cutting off many people; and hast sinned against thy soul."* Hab. ii, 9, 10.

Now, no man can truly know himself, till he be acquainted with this, which is so often the secret and unperceived spring of his actions,

like a soldier serving under him in his wars, than a historian who lived many years afterward, whose business it was to transmit his character impartially to future ages. And in whatever other respects Mr. Dryden may give the preference to Plutarch before Seneca, (which he does with much zeal in his Preface to Plutarch's Lives,) yet it must be allowed that, in this instance, at least, the latter shows more of the philosopher.—See *Plut. Mor.*, vol. i, *ad sin.*

* "O sons of earth! attempt ye still to rise,
By mountains piled on mountains, to the skies?
Heaven still with laughter the vain toil surveys,
And buries madmen in the heaps they raise.
Who wickedly is wise, or madly brave,
Is but the more a fool, or more a knave."

Pope's Essay on Man.

and observes how far it governs and influences him in his conversation and conduct.

And, to correct the irregularity and extravagance of this passion, let us but reflect how airy and unsubstantial a pleasure the highest gratifications of it afford; how many cruel mortifications it exposes us to, by awakening the envy of others; to what meanness it often makes us submit; how frequently it loseth its end, by pursuing it with too much ardour; (for virtue and real excellence will rise to the view of the world, though they be not mounted on the wings of ambition, which, by soaring too high, procures but a more fatal fall;) and how much more solid pleasure the approbation of conscience will yield, than the acclamations of ignorant and mistaken men, who, judging by externals only, cannot know our true character, and whose commendations a wise man would rather despise than court. "Examine but the size of people's sense, and the condition of their understanding, and you will never be fond of popularity, nor afraid of censure; nor solicitous what judgment they may form of you, who know not how to judge rightly of themselves."—*Marc. Anton.*, lib. ix, § 18.

CHAPTER XIII.

What kind of knowledge we are already furnished with, and what degree of esteem we set upon it.

XII. "A MAN can never rightly know himself, unless he examine into his knowledge of other things."

We must consider, then, the knowledge we have; and whether we do not set too high a price upon it, and too great a value upon ourselves on the account of it; of what real use it is to us, and what effect it hath upon us; whether it does not make us too stiff, unsociable, and assuming; testy and supercilious, and ready to despise others for their supposed ignorance. If so, our knowledge, be it what it will, does us more harm than good. We were better without it; ignorance itself would not render us so ridiculous. Such a temper, with all our knowledge, shows that we know not ourselves.

"A man is certainly proud of that knowledge he despises others for the want of."

How common is it for some men to be fond of appearing to know more than they do, and of seeming to be thought men of knowledge! To which end, they exhaust their fund almost in all companies, to outshine the rest; so that, in two or three conversations, they are drawn dry, and you see to the bottom of them much sooner than you could at first imagine. And even that torrent of learning, which they pour upon you at first so unmercifully, rather confounds than satisfies you. Their visible aim is, not to inform your judgment, but display their own. You have many things to query and except against, but their loquacity gives you no room; and their good sense, set off to so much advantage, strikes a modest man dumb. If you insist upon your right to examine, they retreat either in confusion or equivocation; and, like the scuttle-fish, throw a large quantity of ink behind them, that you may not see where to pursue. Whence this foible flows is obvious enough. Self-knowledge would soon correct it.

But, as some ignorantly affect to be more knowing than they are, so others vainly affect to be more ignorant than they are; who, to show they have greater insight and penetration than other men, insist upon the absolute uncertainty of science; will dispute even first principles; grant nothing as certain, and so run into downright Pyrrhonism; the too common effect of abstracted debates excessively refined.

Every one is apt to set the greatest value upon that kind of knowledge in which he imagines he himself most excels, and to undervalue all other kinds of knowledge, in comparison of it. There wants some certain rule, then, by which every man's knowledge is to be tried, and the value of it estimated. And let it be this: "That is the best and most valuable kind of knowledge that is most subservient to the best ends, that is, which tends to make a man wiser and better, or more agreeable and useful both to himself and others." For knowledge is but a means that relates to some end. And as all means are to be judged of by the excellence of their ends, and their expediency to produce them; so, that must be the best knowledge that hath the directest tendency to promote the best ends, namely, a man's own true happiness, and that of others; in which the glory of God, the ultimate end, is ever necessarily comprised.

Now, if we were to judge of the several kinds of science by this rule, we should find, 1. Some of them to be very hurtful and pernicious; as tending to pervert the true end of knowledge; to ruin a man's own happiness, and make him more injurious to society. Such is the knowledge of vice, the various temptations to it, and the secret ways of practising it; especially the arts of dissimulation, fraud, and dishonesty. 2. Others will be found unprofitable and useless, as those parts of knowledge, which, though they may take up much time and pains to acquire, yet answer no valuable purpose; and serve only for amusement, and the entertainment of the imagination: for instance, an acquaintance with plays, novels, games, and modes, in which a man may be very critical and expert, and yet not a whit the wiser or more useful man. 3. Other kinds of knowledge are good only relatively, or conditionally, and may be more useful to one than another; namely, a skill in a man's particular occupation or calling, on which his credit, livelihood, or usefulness in the world depends. And, as this kind of knowledge is valuable in proportion to its end, so it ought to be cultivated with a diligence and esteem answerable to that. Lastly. Other kinds of knowledge are good, absolutely and universally; namely, the knowledge of God and ourselves, the nature of our final happiness, and the way to it. This is equally necessary to all. And how thankful should we be, that we, who live under the light of the gospel, and enjoy that light in its perfection and purity, have so many happy means and opportunities of attaining this most useful and necessary kind of knowledge.

A man can never understand himself, then,

till he makes a right estimate of his knowledge; till he examines what kind of knowledge he values himself most upon, and most diligently cultivates; how high a value he sets upon it; what good it does him; what effect it hath upon him; what he is the better for it; what end it answers now; or what is like to answer hereafter.

There is nothing in which a man's self-ignorance discovers itself more, than in the esteem he hath for his understanding, or for himself on account of it. It is a trite and true observation, "that empty things make the most sound." Men of the least knowledge are most apt to make a show of it, and to value themselves upon it; which is very visible in forward confident youth, raw conceited academics, and those who, uneducated in youth, betake themselves in later life to reading, without taste or judgment, only as an accomplishment, and to make a show of scholarship; who have just learning enough to spoil company, and render themselves ridiculous, but not enough to make either themselves or others at all the wiser.

But, besides the fore-mentioned kinds of knowledge, there is another, which is commonly called false knowledge; which, though it often imposes upon men under the show and semblance of true knowledge, is really worse than ignorance. Some men have learned a great many things, and have taken a great deal of pains to learn them, and stand very high in their own opinion on account of them, which yet they must unlearn before they are truly wise. They have been at a vast expense of time, and pains, and patience, to heap together, and to confirm themselves in a set of wrong notions, which they lay up in their minds as a fund of valuable knowledge; which, if they try by the fore-mentioned rule, namely, "the tendency they have to make them wiser and better, or more useful and beneficial to others," will be found to be worth just nothing at all.

Beware of this false knowledge; for, as there is nothing of which men are more obstinately tenacious, so there is nothing that renders them more vain, or more averse to self-knowledge. Of all things, men are most fond of their wrong notions.

The apostle Paul often speaks of these men, and their self-sufficiency, in very poignant terms; who, "though they seem wise, yet," says he, "must become fools before they are wise," 1 Cor. iii, 18: though they think they know a great deal, "know nothing yet as they ought to know," 1 Cor. viii, 2: but "deceive themselves, by thinking themselves something when they are nothing," Gal. vi, 3: and, while they "desire to be teachers of others, understand not what they say, nor whereof they affirm," 1 Tim. i, 7: and "want themselves to be taught what are the first rudiments and principles of wisdom," Heb. v, 12.

CHAPTER XIV.

Concerning the knowledge, guard, and government of our thoughts.

XIII. "Another part of self-knowledge consists in a due acquaintance with our own thoughts, and the workings of the imagination."

The right government of the thoughts requires no small art, vigilance, and resolution; but it is a matter of such vast importance to the peace and improvement of the mind, that it is worth while to be at some pains about it. A man that hath so numerous and turbulent a family to govern as his own thoughts, which are so apt to be under the influence and command of his passions and appetites, ought not to be long from home: if he is, they will soon grow mutinous and disorderly under the conduct of those two headstrong guides, and raise great clamours and disturbances, and sometimes on the slightest occasions; and a more dreadful scene of misery can hardly be imagined than that which is occasioned by such a tumult and uproar within, when a raging conscience, or inflamed passions, are let loose without check or control. A city in flames, or the mutiny of a drunken crew aboard, who have murdered the captain, and are butchering one another, are but faint emblems of it. The torment of the mind, under such an insurrection and merciless ravage of the passions, is not easy to be conceived. The most revengeful man cannot wish his enemy a greater.

Of what vast importance, then, is it for a man to watch over his thoughts, in order to a right government of them; to consider what kind of thoughts find the easiest admission; in what manner they insinuate themselves, and upon what occasions?

It was an excellent rule which a wise heathen prescribed to himself in his private meditations: "Manage," saith he, "all your actions and thoughts in such a manner, as if you were just going out of the world."—*Marc. Anton. Med.*, lib. ii, § 11. Again, saith he, "A man is seldom, if ever, unhappy for not knowing the thoughts of others; but he that does not attend to the motions of his own, is certainly miserable."—*Marc. Anton.*, lib. ii, § 8.*

It may be worth our while, then, here to discuss this matter a little more particularly; and consider, 1. What kind of thoughts are to be excluded or rejected; and, 2. What ought to be indulged and entertained in the heart.

1. Some thoughts ought to be immediately banished as soon as they have found entrance; and, if we are often troubled with them, the safest way will be to keep a good guard on the avenues of the mind by which they enter, and avoid those occasions which commonly excite them. For, sometimes, it is much easier to prevent a bad thought entering the mind, than to get rid of it when it is entered. More particularly,

(1.) Watch against all fretful and discontented thoughts, which do but chafe and wound the mind to no purpose. To harbour these, is to do yourself more injury than it is in the

* "Nothing can be more unhappy than that man who ranges everywhere, ransacks every thing, digs into the bowels of the earth, dives into other men's bosoms, but does not consider all the while that his own mind will afford him sufficient scope for inquiry and entertainment, and that the care and improvement of himself will give him business enough.

"Your disposition will be suitable to that which you most frequently think on; for the soul is, as it were, tinged with the colour and complexion of its own thoughts."—*Marc. Anton.*

power of your greatest enemy to do you. It is equally a Christian's interest and duty to "learn, in whatever state he is, therewith to be content," Phil. iv, 11.

(2.) Harbour not too anxious and apprehensive thoughts. By giving way to tormenting fears, suspicions of some approaching danger or troublesome event, some not only anticipate, but double the evil they fear; and undergo much more *from the apprehension of it before it comes*, than by suffering it when it is come. This is a great, but common, weakness, which a man should endeavour to arm himself against, by such kind of reflections as these: "Are not all these events under the certain direction of a wise Providence? If they befall me, they are then that share of suffering which God hath appointed me, and which he expects I should bear as a Christian. How often hath my too timorous heart magnified former trials, which I found to be less in reality than they appeared in their approach? And perhaps the formidable aspect they put on is only a stratagem of the great enemy of my best interest, designed on purpose to divert me from some point of duty, or to draw me into some sin, to avoid them. However, why should I torment myself to no purpose? The pain and affliction the dreaded evil will give me, when it comes, is of God's sending; the pain I feel in the apprehension of it, before it comes, is of my own procuring: whereby I often make my sufferings more than double; for this overplus of them, which I bring upon myself, is often greater than that measure of them which the hand of Providence immediately brings upon me."

(3.) Dismiss, as soon as may be, all angry and wrathful thoughts. These will but canker and corrode the mind, and dispose it to the worst temper in the world, namely, that of fixed malice and revenge. "Anger may steal into the heart of a wise man, but it rests only in the bosom of fools," Eccles. vii, 9. Make all the most candid allowances for the offender; consider his natural temper; turn your anger into pity; repeat 1 Cor. xiii; think of the patience and meekness of Christ, and the petition in the Lord's prayer; and how much you stand in need of forgiveness yourself, both from God and man; how fruitless, how foolish, is indulged resentment; how tormenting to yourself. You have too much good nature willingly to give others so much torment; and why should you give it yourself? You are commanded to love your neighbour as yourself, but not forbidden to love yourself as much. And why should you do yourself that injury which your enemy would be glad to do you?* Especially,

(4.) Banish all malignant and revengeful thoughts. A spirit of revenge is the very spirit of the devil; than which, nothing makes a man more like him, and nothing can be more opposite to the temper which Christianity was designed to promote. If your revenge be not satisfied, it will give you torment now; if it be, it will give you greater hereafter. None is a greater self-tormentor than a malicious and revengeful man, who turns the poison of his own temper in upon himself.

(5.) Drive from the mind all silly, trifling, and unseasonable thoughts; which sometimes get into it we know not how, and seize and possess it before we are aware, and hold it in empty idle amusements, that yield it neither pleasure nor profit, and turn to no manner of account in the world, only consume time, and prevent a better employment of the mind. And, indeed, there is little difference, whether we

* The Christian precept in this case is, "Let not the sun go down upon your wrath," Eph. iv, 26. And this precept Plutarch tells us the Pythagoreans practised in a literal sense: "Who, if at any time in a passion they broke out into opprobrious language, before sunset gave one another their hands, and with them a discharge from all injuries; and so with a mutual reconciliation parted friends."

spend the time in sleep, or in these waking dreams. Nay, if the thoughts which thus insensibly steal upon you be not altogether absurd and whimsical, yet, if they be impertinent and unseasonable, they ought to be dismissed, because they keep out better company.

(6.) Cast out all wild and extravagant thoughts, all vain and fantastical imaginations. Suffer not your thoughts to roam upon things that never were, and perhaps never will be ; to give you a visionary pleasure in the prospect of what you have not the least reason to hope, or a needless pain in the apprehension of what you have not the least reason to fear. The truth is, next to a clear conscience, and a sound judgment, there is not a greater blessing than a regular and well-governed imagination; to be able to view things as they are, in their true light and proper colours; and to distinguish the false images that are painted on the fancy from the representations of truth and reason. For, how common a thing is it for men, before they are aware, to confound reason and fancy, truth and imagination, together? to take the flashes of the animal spirits for the light of evidence; and think they believe things to be true or false, when they only fancy them to be so, because they would have them so? not considering that mere fancy is only the *ignis fatuus* of the mind; which often appears brightest when the mind is most covered with darkness, and will be sure to lead them astray who follow it as their guide. Near akin to these are,

(7.) Romantic and chimerical thoughts. By which I mean that kind of wild-fire which the briskness of the animal spirits sometimes suddenly flashes upon the mind, and excites images that are so extremely ridiculous and absurd, that one can scarce forbear wondering how they could get admittance. These random flights of fancy are soon gone ; and so differ from that castle-building of the imagination before-mentioned, which is a more settled amusement. But these are too incoherent and senseless to be of long continuance ; and are the maddest sallies, and the most ramping reveries of the fancy that can be. I know not whether my reader understands now what I mean ; but if he attentively regards all that passes through his mind, perhaps he may, hereafter, by experience.

(8.) Repel all impure and lascivious thoughts, which taint and pollute the mind ; and though hid from men, are known to God, in whose eye they are abominable. Our Saviour warns us against these, as a kind of spiritual fornication,

(Matt. v, 28,) and inconsistent with that purity of heart which his gospel requires.

(9.) Take care how you too much indulge gloomy and melancholy thoughts. Some are disposed to see every thing in the worst light. A black cloud hangs hovering over their minds, which, when it falls in showers through the eyes, is dispersed, and all within is serene again. This is often purely mechanical; and owing, either to some fault in the bodily constitution, or some accidental disorder in the animal frame. However, one that consults the peace of his own mind, will be upon his guard against this, which so often robs him of it.

(10.) On the other hand, let not the imagination be too sprightly and triumphant. Some are as unreasonably exalted as others are depressed; and the same person, at different times, often runs into both extremes, according to the different temper and flow of the animal spirits. And therefore the thoughts which so eagerly crowd into the mind at such times ought to be suspected and well guarded, otherwise they will impose upon our judgments, and lead us to form such a notion of ourselves, and of things, which we shall soon see fit to alter, when the mind is in a more settled and sedate frame.

Before we let our thoughts judge of things,

we must set reason to judge our thoughts; for they are not always in a proper condition to execute that office. We do not believe the character which a man gives us of another, unless we have a good opinion of his own; so, neither should we believe the verdict which the mind pronounces, till we first examine, whether it be impartial and unbiased; whether it be in a proper temper to judge, and have proper lights to judge by. The want of this previous act of self-judgment is the cause of so much self-deception and false judgment.

Lastly, with abhorrence reject immediately all profane and blasphemous thoughts, which are sometimes suddenly injected into the mind, we know not how, though we may give a pretty good guess from whence. And all those thoughts, which are apparently temptations and inducements to sin, our Lord hath, by his example, taught us to treat in this manner. Matt. iv, 10.

These, then, are the thoughts we should carefully guard against. And as they will (especially some of them) be frequently insinuating themselves into the heart, remember to set reason at the door of it to guard the passage, and bar their entrance, or drive them out forthwith when entered; not only as impertinent, but mischievous intruders.

But, II. There are other kinds of thoughts which we ought to indulge, and with great care and diligence retain and improve.

Whatever thoughts give the mind a rational or religious pleasure, and tend to improve the heart and understanding, are to be favoured, often recalled, and carefully cultivated. Nor should we dismiss them till they have made some impressions on the mind which are like to abide there.

And to bring the mind into a habit of recovering, retaining, and improving such thoughts, two things are necessary.

1. To habituate ourselves to a close and rational way of thinking. And, 2. To moral reflections and religious contemplations.

(1). To prepare and dispose the mind for the entertainment of good and useful thoughts, we must take care to habituate it to a close and rational way of thinking.

When you have started a good thought, pursue it; do not presently lose sight of it, or suffer any trifling suggestion that may intervene to divert you from it. Dismiss it not till you have sifted and exhausted it, and well considered the several consequences and inferences that result from it. However, retain not the subject any longer than you find your thoughts run freely upon it; for, to confine them to it when it is quite worn out, is to give them an unnatural bent, without sufficient employment; which will make them flag, or be more apt to run off to something else.

And, to keep the mind intent on the subject you think of, you must be at some pains to recall and refix your desultory and rambling thoughts. Lay open the subject in as many lights and views as it is capable of being represented in; clothe your best ideas in pertinent and well-chosen words, deliberately pronounced; or commit them to writing.

Whatever be the subject, admit of no inferences from it, but what you see plain and natural. This is the way to furnish the mind with true and solid knowledge, as, on the contrary, false knowledge proceeds from not understanding the subject, or drawing inferences from it which are forced and unnatural, and allowing to those precarious inferences, or consequences drawn from them, the same degree of credibility as to the most rational and best-established principles.

Beware of a superficial, slight, or confused view of things. Go to the bottom of them, and examine the foundation; and be satisfied with none but clear and distinct ideas (when they can be had) in every thing you read, hear, or think of. For, resting in imperfect and obscure ideas, is the source of much confusion and mistake.

Accustom yourself to speak naturally, pertinently, and rationally on all subjects, and you will soon learn to think so on the best; especially if you often converse with those persons that speak, and those authors that write, in that manner.

And such a regulation and right management of your thoughts and rational powers will be of great and general advantage to you, in the pursuit of useful knowledge, and a good guard against the levities and frantic sallies of the imagination. Nor will you be sensible of any disadvantage attending it, excepting one, namely, its making you more sensible of the weakness and ignorance of others, who are often talking in a random, inconsequential manner; and whom, however, it may oftentimes be more prudent to bear with than contradict. But the vast benefit this method will be of in tracing out truth, and detecting error, and the satisfaction it will give you in the cool and regular exercises of self-employment, and in the retaining, pursuing, and improving good and useful thoughts, will more than compensate that petty disadvantage.

(2.) If we would have the mind furnished and entertained with good thoughts, we must inure it to moral and religious subjects.

It is certain the mind cannot be more nobly or usefully employed than in such kind of contemplations: because the knowledge it thereby acquires is, of all other, the most excellent knowledge, and that both in regard to its object and its end; the object of it being God, and the end of it eternal happiness.

The great end of religion is, to "make us like God, and conduct us to the enjoyment of him." And whatever hath not this plain tendency, and especially if it have the contrary, men may call religion, if they please; but they cannot call it more out of its name. And whatever is called religious knowledge, if it does not direct us in the way to this end, is not religious knowledge, but something else, falsely so called. And some are unhappily accustomed to such an abuse of words and understanding, as not only to call, but to think, those things religion, which are the very reverse of it; and those notions religious knowledge, which lead them the furthest from it.

The sincerity of a true religious principle cannot be better known, than by the readiness with which the thoughts advert to God, and the pleasure with which they are employed in devout exercises. And though a person may not always be so well pleased with hearing religious things talked of by others, whose different taste, sentiments, or manner of expression, may have something disagreeable; yet, if he have no inclination to think of them himself, or converse with himself about them, he hath great reason to suspect that his "heart is not right with God." But, if he frequently and delightfully exercises his mind in divine contemplations, it will not only be a good mark of his sincerity, but will habitually dispose it for the reception of the best and most useful thoughts, and fit it for the noblest entertainments.

Upon the whole, then, it is of as great importance for a man to take heed what thoughts he entertains, as what company he keeps; for they have the same effect upon the mind. Bad thoughts are as infectious as bad company; and good thoughts solace, instruct, and entertain the mind, like good company. And this is one great advantage of retirement; that a man may choose what company he pleases, from within himself.

As, in the world, we oftener light into bad company than good; so, in solitude, we are oftener troubled with impertinent and unprofitable thoughts, than entertained with agreeable and useful ones. And a man that hath so far lost the command of himself, as to lie at the mercy of every foolish or vexing thought, is much in the same situation as a host, whose house is open to all comers, whom, though ever so noisy, rude, and troublesome, he cannot get rid of: but with this difference, that the latter hath some recompense for his trouble, the former none at all, but is robbed of his peace and quiet for nothing.

Of such vast importance to the peace, as well as the improvement of the mind, is the right regulation of the thoughts, which will be my apology for dwelling so long on this branch of the subject, which I shall conclude with this one observation more; that it is a very dangerous thing to think, as too many are apt to do, that it is a matter of indifference what thoughts they entertain in their hearts, since the reason of things concurs with the testimony of the Holy Scriptures to assure us, "that the allowed thought of foolishness is sin," Prov. xxvi, 9.

CHAPTER XV.

Concerning the memory.

XIV. "A MAN that knows himself will have a regard, not only to the management of his thoughts, but the improvement of his memory."

The memory is that faculty of the soul which was designed for the storehouse or repository of its most useful notions; where they may be laid up in safety, to be produced on proper occasions.

Now, a thorough self-acquaintance cannot be had without a proper regard to this in two respects: (1.) Its furniture. (2.) Its improvement.

(1.) A man that knows himself will have a regard to the furniture of his memory; not to load it with trash and lumber, a set of useless notions, or low conceits, which he will be ashamed to produce before persons of taste and judgment.

If the retention be bad, do not crowd it. It is of as ill consequence to overload a weak memory as a weak stomach. And, that it may not be cumbered with trash, take heed what company you keep, what books you read, and what thoughts you favour; otherwise a great deal of useless rubbish may fix there before you are aware, and take up the room which ought to be possessed by better notions. But let not a valuable thought slip from you, though you pursue it with much time and pains before you overtake it. The regaining and refixing it may be of more avail to you than many hours, reading.

What pity is it that men should take such immense pains, as some do, to learn those things, which, as soon as they become wise, they must take as much pains to unlearn! A thought that should make us very curious and cautious about the proper furniture of our minds.

(2.) Self-knowledge will acquaint a man with the extent and capacity of his memory, and the right way to improve it.

There is no small art in improving a weak memory, so as to turn it to as great an advantage as many do theirs, which are much stronger. A few short rules to this purpose may be no unprofitable digression.

1. Beware of all kinds of intemperance in the indulgence of the appetites and passions. Excesses of all kinds do a great injury to the memory.

2. If it be weak, do not overload it. Charge it only with the most useful and solid notions.

A small vessel should not be stuffed with lumber: but if its freight be precious, and judiciously stowed, it may be more valuable than a ship of twice its burden.

3. Recur to the help of a common-place book, according to Mr. Locke's method, and review it once a year. But take care, that, by confiding to your minutes or memorial aids, you do not excuse the labour of the memory ; which is one disadvantage attending this method.

4. Take every opportunity of uttering your best thoughts in conversation, when the subject will admit it: that will deeply imprint them. Hence, the tales which common story-tellers relate, they never forget, though ever so silly.

5. Join, to the idea you would remember, some other that is more familiar to you, which bears some similitude to it, either in its nature or in the sound of the word by which it is expressed ; or that hath some relation to it, either in time or place. And then by recalling this, which is easily remembered, you will (by that concatenation or connection of ideas, which Mr. Locke takes notice of) draw in that which is thus linked or joined with it; which otherwise you might hunt after in vain. This rule is of excellent use to help you to remember names.

6. What you are determined to remember, think of before you go to sleep at night, and the first thing in the morning, when the faculties are fresh. And recollect, at evening, every thing worth remembering the day past.

7. Think it not enough to furnish this storehouse of the mind with good thoughts; but lay them up there in order, digested or ranged under proper subjects or classes; that, whatever subject you have occasion to think or talk upon, you may have recourse immediately to a good thought, which you heretofore laid up there under that subject, so that the very mention of the subject may bring the thought to hand; by which means you will carry a regular commonplace book in your memory. And it may not be amiss, sometimes, to take an inventory of this mental furniture, and recollect how many good thoughts you have there treasured up under such particular subjects, and whence you had them.

Lastly. Nothing helps the memory more than often thinking, writing, or talking, on those subjects you would remember. But enough of this.

CHAPTER XVI.

Concerning the mental taste.

XV. "A MAN that knows himself is sensible of, and attentive to, the particular taste of his mind, especially in matters of religion."

As the late Mr. Howe judiciously observes, "there is, besides bare understanding and judgment, and diverse from that heavenly gift, which, in the Scripture, is called grace, such a thing as gust and relish belonging to the mind of man, (and, I doubt not, with all men, if they observe themselves,) and which are as unaccountable, and as various, as the relishes and disgusts of sense. This they only wonder at who understand not themselves, or will consider nobody but themselves. So that it cannot be said universally, that it is a better judgment, or more grace, that determines men the one way or the other; but somewhat in the temper of their minds distinct from both, which I know not how better to express than by mental taste. And this hath no more of mystery in it, than that there is such a thing belonging to our natures as complacency and displacency in reference to the objects of the mind. And this, in the kind of it, is as common to men as human nature; but as much diversified in individuals as men's other inclinations are."

Now, this different taste in matters relating to religion, (though it may be sometimes natural, or what is born with a man, yet,) generally arises from the difference of education and custom. And the true reason why some persons have an inveterate disrelish to certain circumstantials of religion, though ever so justifiable, and at the same time a fixed esteem for others that are more exceptionable, may be no better than what I have heard some very honestly profess, namely, that the one they have been used to, and the other not. As a person, by long use and habit, acquires a greater relish for coarse and unwholesome food, than the most delicate diet; so a person long habituated to a set of phrases, notions, and modes, may, by degrees, come to have such a veneration and esteem for them, as to despise and condemn others which they have not been accustomed to, though perhaps more edifying and more agreeable to Scripture and reason.

This particular taste in matters of religion differs very much (as Mr. Howe well observes) both from judgment and grace.

However, it is often mistaken for both. When it is mistaken for the former, it leads to error; when mistaken for the latter, to censoriousness.

This different taste of mental objects is much the same with that which, with regard to the objects of sense, we call fancy: for, as one man cannot be said to have a better judgment in food than another, purely because he likes some kind of meats better than he; so neither can he be said to have a better judgment in matters of religion, purely because he hath a greater fondness for some particular doctrines and forms.

But though this mental taste be not the same as the judgment, yet it often draws the judgment to it, and sometimes very much perverts it.

This appears in nothing more evidently than in the judgment people pass upon the sermons they hear. Some are best pleased with those discourses that are pathetic and warming, others with what is more solid and rational, and others with the sublime and mystical. Nothing can be too plain for the taste of some, or too refined for that of others. Some are for having the address only to their reason and understanding, others only to their affections and passions, and others to their experience and conscience. And every hearer, or reader, is apt to judge according to his particular taste, and to esteem him the best preacher or writer who pleases him most; without examining, first, his own particular taste, by which he judgeth.

It is natural, indeed, for every one to desire to have his own taste pleased; but it is unreasonable in him to set it up as the best, and make it a test and standard to others; but much more unreasonable to expect, that he who speaks in public should always speak to his taste, which might as reasonably be expected by another of a different taste. But it can no more be expected, that what is delivered to a multitude of hearers should alike suit all their tastes, than that a single dish, though prepared with ever so much art and exactness, should equally please a great variety of appetites; among which there may be some, perhaps, very nice and sickly.

It is the preacher's duty to adapt his subjects to the taste of his hearers, as far as fidelity and conscience will admit; because it is well known, from reason and experience, as well as from the advice and practice of the apostle Paul,*

* Rom. xv, 2: "Let every one of us please his neighbour for his good to edification." 1 Cor. ix, 22: "To the weak became I as weak, that I might gain the weak: I am made all things to all men, that I might by all means save some."

that this is the best way to promote their edification. But if their taste be totally vitiated, and incline them to take in that which will do them more harm than good, and to relish poison more than food, the most charitable thing the preacher can do in that case is to endeavour to correct so vicious an appetite, which loathes that which is most wholesome, and craves that which is pernicious. This, I say, it is his duty to attempt in the most gentle and prudent manner he can, though he run the risk of having his judgment or orthodoxy called into question by them, as it very possibly may; for, commonly, they are the most arbitrary and unmerciful judges in this case who are the least able to judge.

There is not, perhaps, a more unaccountable weakness in human nature than this, that, with regard to religious matters, our animosities are generally greatest where our differences are least: they who come pretty near to our standard, but stop short there, are more the object of our disgust and censure, than they who continue at the greatest distance from it; and it requires the greatest knowledge and command of our temper to get over this weakness. To whatever secret spring in the human mind it may be owing, I shall not stay to inquire; but the thing itself is too obvious not to be taken notice of.

Now, we should, all of us, be careful to find out and examine our proper taste of religious things; that, if it be a false one, we may rectify it; if a bad one, mend it; if a right and good one, strengthen and improve it. For the mind is capable of a false taste, as well as the palate, and comes by it the same way, namely, by being long used to unnatural relishes, which, by custom, become grateful. And having found out what it is, and examined it by the test of Scripture, reason, and conscience, if it be not very wrong, let us indulge it, and read those books that are most suited to it, which, for that reason, will be most edifying. But, at the same time, let us take care of two things: 1. That it do not bias our judgment, and draw us into error. 2. That it do not cramp our charity, and lead us to censoriousness.

CHAPTER XVII.

Of our great and governing views in life.

XVI. "Another part of self-knowledge is, to know what are the great ends for which we live."

We must consider what is the ultimate scope we drive at; the general maxims and principles we live by; or whether we have not yet determined our end, and are governed by no fixed principles, or by such as we are ashamed to own.

There are few that live so much at random as not to have some main end in eye; something that influences their conduct, and is the great object of their pursuit and hope. A man cannot live without some leading views; a wise man will always know what they are; whether it is fit he should be led by them, or no; whether they be such as his understanding and reason approve, or only such as fancy and inclination suggest. He will be as much concerned to act with reason, as to talk with reason; as much ashamed of a solecism and contradiction in his character, as in his conversation.

Where do our views centre? In this world we are in, or in that we are going to? If our hopes and joys centre here, it is a mortifying thought, that we are every day "departing from our happiness;" but if they are fixed above, it is a joy to think, that we are every day drawing nearer to the object of our highest wishes.

Is our main care to appear great in the eye of man, or good in the eye of God? If the former, we expose ourselves to the pain of a perpetual disappointment; for it is much, if the envy of men do not rob us of a great deal of our just praise, or if our vanity will be content with that they allow us. But if the latter be our main care; if our chief view is to be approved of God, we are laying up a fund of the most lasting and solid satisfactions: not to say that this is the truest way to appear great in the eye of men, and to conciliate the esteem of all those whose praise is worth our wish.

"Be this, then, O my soul! thy wise and steady pursuit; let this circumscribe and direct thy views; be this a law to thee, from which account it a sin to depart, whatever disrespect or contempt it may expose thee to from others;*

* "What you have once wisely purposed stick to, as a law

be this the character thou resolvest to live up to, and at all times to maintain, both in public and private, namely, a friend and lover of God ; in whose favour thou centrest all thy present and future hopes. Carry this view with thee through life, and dare not, in any instance, to act inconsistently with it."

CHAPTER XVIII.

How to know the true state of our souls ; and whether we are fit to die.

Lastly. "The most important point of self-knowledge, after all, is, to know the true state of our souls toward God, and in what condition we are to die."

These two things are inseparably connected in their nature, and therefore I put them together. The knowledge of the former will determine the latter, and is the only thing than can determine it ; for no man can tell whether he is fit for death, till he is acquainted with the true state of his own soul.

not to be violated without guilt. And mind not what others say of you.

"Fix your character, and keep to it ; whether alone or in company."—*Epictetus.*

This, now, is a matter of such vast moment, that it is amazing any considerate man, or any one who thinks what it is to die, should rest satisfied with an uncertainty in it. Let us trace out this important point, then, with all possible plainness, and see if we cannot come to some satisfaction in it upon the most solid principles.

In order to know, then, whether we are fit to die, we must first know, "what is it that fits us for death?" And the answer to this is very natural and easy; namely, "that only fits us for death that fits us for happiness after death."

This is certain. But the question returns: "What is it that fits us for happiness after death?"

Now, in answer to this, there is a previous question necessary to be determined, namely, "What that happiness is?"

It is not a fool's paradise, or a Turkish dream of sensitive gratifications; it must be a happiness suited to the nature of the soul, and what it is capable of enjoying in a state of separation from the body. And what can that be, but the enjoyment of God, the best of beings, and the author of ours?

The question, then, comes to this, "What is that which fits us for the enjoyment of God, in the future state of separate spirits?"

And, methinks, we may bring this matter to a very sure and short issue, by saying, it is "that which makes us like to him now." This only is our proper qualification for the enjoyment of him after death, and therefore our only proper preparation for death. For how can they who are unlike to God here, expect to enjoy him hereafter? And if they have no just ground to hope that they shall enjoy God in the other world, how are they fit to die?

So that the great question, "Am I fit to die?" resolves itself into this, "Am I like to God?" for it is this only that fits me for heaven; and that which fits me for heaven is the only thing that fits me for death.

Let this point, then, be well searched into, and examined very deliberately and impartially.

Most certain it is, that God can take no real complacency in any but those that are like him; and it is as certain, that none but those that are like him can take pleasure in him. But God is a most pure and holy being; a being of infinite love, mercy, and patience; whose righteousness is invariable, whose veracity is inviolable, and whose wisdom unerring. These are the moral attributes of the divine Being, in which he requires us to imitate him; the express lineaments of the divine nature, in which all good men bear a resemblance to him, and for the sake of which only they are the objects of his delight: for God can love none but those that bear this impress of his own image on their souls. Do we find, then, these visible traces of the divine image there? Can we make out our likeness to him in his holiness, goodness, mercy, righteousness, truth, and wisdom? If so, it is certain we are capable of enjoying him, and are the proper objects of his love. By this we know we are fit to die, because, by this we know we are fit for happiness after death.

Thus, then, if we are faithful to our consciences, and impartial in the examination of our lives and tempers, we may soon come to a right determination of this important question, "What is the true state of our souls toward God, and in what condition are we to die?"*

* "Nor do I apprehend the knowledge of our state (call it assurance, if you please) so uncommon and extraordinary a thing as some are apt to imagine. Understand by assurance a satisfactory evidence of the thing, such as excludes all reasonable doubts and disquieting fears of the contrary, though, it may be, not all transient suspicions and jealousies. And

Which, as it is the most important, so it is the last instance of self-knowledge I shall mention, and with it close the first part of this subject.

such an assurance and certainty multitudes have attained, and enjoy the comfort of: and indeed it is of so high importance, that it is a wonder any thoughtful Christian that believes an eternity can be easy one day or week without it."

Bennett's Christ. Orat., p. 569.

A TREATISE

ON

SELF-KNOWLEDGE.

PART II.

Showing the great excellence and advantages of this kind of science.

Having, in the former part of the subject, laid open some of the main branches of self-knowledge, or pointed out the principal things which a man ought to be acquainted with, relating to himself, I am now, reader, to lay before you the excellence and usefulness of this kind of knowledge, as an inducement to labour after it, by a detail of the several great advantages which attend it, and which shall be recounted in the following chapters.

CHAPTER I

Self-knowledge the spring of self-possession.

"I. ONE great advantage of self-knowledge is, that it gives a man the truest and most constant self-possession."

A man that is endowed with this excellent knowledge is calm and easy :—

(1.) Under affronts and defamation. For he thinks thus : "I am sure I know myself better than any man can pretend to know me. This calumniator hath, indeed, at this time, missed his mark, and shot his arrows at random ; and it is my comfort, that my conscience acquits me of his angry imputation. However, there are worse crimes which he might more justly accuse me of, which, though hid from him, are known to myself. Let me set about reforming them, lest, if they come to his notice, he should attack me in a more defenceless part, find something to fasten his obloquy, and fix a lasting reproach on my character."*

There is a great deal of truth and good sense

* "If you are told that another reviles you, do not go about to vindicate yourself, but reply thus : My other faults I find are hidden from him, else I should have heard of them too."—*Epictetus.*

in that common saying and doctrine of the Stoics, though they might carry it too far, that "it is not things, but thoughts, that disturb and hurt us."* Now, a self-acquaintance teaches a man the right government of the thoughts, (as is shown above, part i, chap. 14,) it will help him to expel all anxious, tormenting, and fruitless thoughts, and retain the most quieting and useful ones, and so keep all easy within. Let a man but try the experiment, and he will find that a little resolution will make the greatest part of the difficulty vanish.

(2.) Self-knowledge will be a good ballast to the mind under any accidental hurry or disorder of the passions. It curbs their impetuosity, puts the reins into the hands of reason, quells the rising storm, ere it make shipwreck of the conscience, and teaches a man to "leave off contention before it be meddled with," Prov. xvii, 14; it being much safer to keep the lion

* "It is not things, but men's opinion of things that disturbs them. Remember, it is not he that reviles or assaults you, that injures you, but your thinking that he has injured you. No man can hurt you, unless you permit him: then only are you hurt when you think yourself so.

"Things do not touch the mind, but stand quietly without he vexation comes from within, from our suspicions only. Things themselves cannot affect the mind: for they have no entrance into it, to turn and move it. It is the mind alone that turns and moves itself."—*Epictetus.*

chained than to encounter it in its full strength and fury. And thus will a wise man for his own peace deal with the passions of others, as well as his own.

Self-knowledge, as it acquaints a man with his weaknesses and worst qualities, will be his guard against them, and a happy counterbalance to the faults and excesses of his natural temper.

(3.) It will keep the mind sedate and calm under the surprise of bad news, or afflicting providences.

"For, am I not a creature of God? and my life and my comforts, are they not wholly at his dispose, from whom I have received them, and by whose favour I have so long enjoyed them, and by whose mercy and goodness I have still so many left me?

"A heathen can teach me, under such losses of friends, or estate, or any comfort, to direct my eyes to the hand of God, by whom it was lent me, and is now recalled, that I ought not to say, it is lost, but restored; and though I be injuriously deprived of it, still the hand of God is to be acknowledged; for, what is it to me by what means he that gave me that blessing takes it from me again?"—*Epict. Enchirid.*, cap. 15.

He that rightly knows himself, will live

every day dependant on the divine Author of his mercies, for the continuance and enjoyment of them; and will learn, from a higher authority than that of a heathen moralist, that he hath nothing that he can properly call his own, or ought to depend upon as such; that he is but a steward employed to dispense the good things he possesses, according to the direction of his Lord, at whose pleasure he holds them, and to whom he should be ready, at any time, cheerfully to resign them. Luke xvi, 1.

(4.) Self-knowledge will help a man to preserve an equanimity and self-possession under all the various scenes of adversity and prosperity.

Both have their temptations. To some, the temptations of prosperity are the greatest; to others, those of adversity. Self-knowledge shows a man which of these are greatest to him; and, at the apprehension of them, teaches him to arm himself accordingly, that nothing may deprive him of his constancy and self-possession, or lead him to act unbecoming the man or the Christian.

We commonly say, "No one knows what he can bear, till he is tried." And many persons verify the observation, by bearing evils much better than they feared they should. Nay, the apprehension of an approaching evil often gives a man a greater pain than the evil itself. This is owing to inexperience and self-ignorance.

A man that knows himself, his own strength and weakness, is not so subject as others to the melancholy presages of the imagination; and, whenever they intrude, he makes no other use of them than to take the warning, collect himself, and prepare for the coming evil; leaving the degree, duration, and the issue of it with him who is the sovereign Disposer of all events, in a quiet dependance on his power, wisdom, and goodness.

Such self-possession is one great effect and advantage of self-knowledge.

CHAPTER II.

Self-knowledge leads to a wise and steady conduct.

II. "As self-knowledge will keep a man calm and equal in his temper, so it will make him wise and cautious in his conduct."

A precipitant and rash conduct is ever the effect of a confused and irregular hurry of the thoughts. So that, when, by the influence of self-knowledge, the thoughts become cool, sedate, and rational, the conduct will be so too. It will give a man that even, steady, uniform behaviour in the management of his affairs, that is so necessary for the despatch of business, and prevent many disappointments and troubles, which arise from the unsuccessful execution of immature or ill-judged projects.

In short, most of the troubles which men meet with in the world may be traced up to this source, and resolved into self-ignorance. We may complain of Providence, and complain of men ; but the fault, if we examine it, will commonly be found to be our own. Our imprudence, which arises from self-ignorance, either brings our troubles upon us, or increases them. Want of temper and conduct will make any affliction double.

What a long train of difficulties do sometimes proceed from one wrong step in our conduct, which self-ignorance, or inconsideration, betrayed us into ! And every evil that befalls us, in consequence of that, we are to charge upon ourselves.

CHAPTER III.

Humility the effect of self-knowledge.

III. "TRUE self-knowledge always produces humility."

Pride is ever the offspring of self-ignorance. The reason men are vain and self-sufficient is, because they do not know their own failings; and the reason they are not better acquainted with them is, because they hate self-inspection. Let a man but turn his eyes within, scrutinize himself, and study his own heart, and he will soon see enough to make him humble. "Behold, I am vile," (Job xl, 4,) is the language only of self-knowledge.

Whence is it that young people are generally so vain, self-sufficient, and assured, but because they have taken no time or pains to cultivate a self-acquaintance? And why does pride and stiffness appear so often in advanced age, but because men grow old in self-ignorance? A moderate degree of self-knowledge would cure an inordinate degree of self-complacency.

Humility is not more necessary to salvation, than self-knowledge is to humility.

And especially would it prevent that bad disposition which is too apt to steal upon and infect some of the best human minds, especially those who aim at singular and exalted degrees of piety, namely, a religious vanity, or spiritual pride; which, without a great deal of self-knowledge and self-attention, will gradually insinuate into the heart, taint the mind, and sophisticate our virtues, before we are aware; and, in proportion to its prevalence, make the Christian temper degenerate into the pharisaical.

"Might I be allowed to choose my own lot, I should think it much more eligible to want my spiritual comforts, than to abound in these, at the expense of my humility. No; let a penitent and contrite spirit be always my portion; and may I ever so be the favourite of Heaven as never to forget that I am chief of sinners. Knowledge in the sublime and glorious mysteries of the Christian faith, and ravishing contemplations of God and a future state, are most desirable advantages; but still I prefer charity, which edifieth, before the highest intellectual perfections of that knowledge which puffeth up. 1 Cor. viii, 1. Those spiritual advantages are certainly best for us which increase our modesty and awaken our caution, and dispose us to suspect and deny ourselves. The highest in God's esteem are meanest in their own; and their excellence consists in the meekness and truth, not in the pomp and ostentation of piety, which affects to be seen and admired of men."*—*Stanhope's Thomas à Kempis*, book ii, chap. 11.

* In the same work Christ is supposed to address his disciple in the following words: "My son, when thou feelest thy soul warmed with devotion and holy zeal for my service, it will be advisable to decline all those methods of publishing it to the world, which vain men are so industrious to take, and content thyself with its being known to God and thine own conscience. Rather endeavour to moderate and suppress those pompous expressions of it, in which some place the very perfection of zeal. Think meanly of thy own virtues. Some men of a bold ungoverned zeal aspire at things beyond their strength, and express more vehemence than conduct in their actions. They are perfectly carried out of themselves with eagerness; forget that they are still poor insects upon earth, and think of nothing less than building their nest in heaven. Virtue does not consist in abundance of illumination and knowledge; but in lowliness of mind, in meekness and charity; in a mind entirely resigned to God, and sincerely disposed to serve and please him.

"It is a dangerous drunkenness, I confess, that of wine; but there is another more dangerous. How many persons do I see in the world drunk with vanity, and a high opinion of themselves! This drunkenness causes them to make a thousand false steps and a thousand stumbles. Their ways are all oblique and crooked. Like men in drink, they have always a great opinion of their own wisdom, their power and their prudence: all which often fail them. Examine well thyself, my soul: see if thou art not tainted with this evil."

CHAPTER IV.

Charity another effect of self-knowledge.

IV. "SELF-KNOWLEDGE greatly promotes a spirit of meekness and charity."

The more a man is acquainted with his own failings, the more is he disposed to make allowances for those of others. The knowledge he hath of himself will incline him to be as severe in his animadversions on his own conduct as he is on that of others, and as candid to their faults as he is to his own.*

There is an uncommon beauty, force, and propriety, in that caution which our Saviour gives us, Matt. vii, 3–5: "And why beholdest thou the mote that is in thy brother's eye, but considerest not the beam that is in thine own eye? Or how wilt thou say to thy brother, Let me pull out the mote out of thine eye, and behold a beam is in thine own eye? Thou hypocrite, first cast the beam out of thine own eye, and then shalt thou see clearly to cast out the mote out of thy brother's eye." In which

* "The great God seems to have given that commandment, KNOW THYESLF, to those men more especially who are apt to make remarks on other men's actions, and forget themselves."—*Plutarch.*

words these four things are plainly intimated: 1. That some are much more quick-sighted to discern the faults and blemishes of others than their own; can spy a mote in another's eye sooner than a beam in their own: and commonly it is so; they who are most quick-sighted to the faults of others, are most blind to their own. 2. That they are often the most forward and officious to correct and cure the foibles of others, who are most unfit for it. The beam in their own eye makes them altogether unfit to pull out the mote from their brother's. A man, half blind himself, should never set up for an oculist. 3. That they who are inclined to deal in censure should always begin at home. 4. Great censoriousness is great hypocrisy. "Thou hypocrite," &c., all this is nothing but the effect of woful self-ignorance.

This common failing of the human nature the heathens were very sensible of, and represented it in the following manner. Every man, say they, carries a wallet, or two bags, with him; the one hanging before him, the other behind him: in that before, he puts the faults of others; into that behind, his own; by which means, he never sees his own failings, while he has those of others always before his eyes.

But self-knowledge, now, helps us to turn

this wallet, and place that which hath our own faults before our eyes, and that which hath in it those of others behind our back. A very necessary regulation this, if we would behold our own faults in the same light in which they do; for we must not expect that others will be as blind to our foibles as we ourselves are; they will carry them before their eyes, whether we do or no. And to imagine that the world takes no notice of them, because we do not, is just as wise as to fancy that others do not see us, because we shut our eyes.

CHAPTER V.

Moderation the effect of self-knowledge.

V. "ANOTHER genuine offspring of self-knowledge is moderation."

This, indeed, can hardly be conceived to be separate from that meekness and charity before mentioned; but I choose to give it a distinct mention, because I consider it under a different view and operation, namely, as that which guards and influences our spirits in all matters of debate and controversy.

Moderation is a great and important Christian virtue, very different from that bad quality of the mind under which it is often misrepresented and disguised, namely, lukewarmness and indifference about the truth. The former is very consistent with a regular and well-corrected zeal; the latter consists in the total want of it: the former is sensible of, and endeavours, with peace and prudence, to maintain the dignity and importance of divine doctrines; the latter hath no manner of concern about them: the one feels the secret influences of them; the other is quite a stranger to their power and efficacy: the one laments, in secret, the sad decay of vital religion; the other is an instance of it. In short, the one proceeds from true knowledge, the other from great ignorance; the one is a good mark of sincerity, the other a certain sign of hypocrisy. And to confound two things together which are so essentially different, can be the effect of nothing but great ignorance, or inconsideration, or an over-heated, injudicious zeal.

A self-knowing man can easily distinguish between these two. And the knowledge which he has of human nature in general, from a thorough contemplation of his own in particular, shows him the necessity of preserving a medium (as in every thing else, so especially) between the two extremes of a bigoted zeal on the one hand, and an indolent lukewarmness on the other. As he will not look upon every thing to be worth contending for, so he will look upon nothing worth losing his temper for in the contention; because, though the truth be of ever so great importance, nothing can be of a greater disservice to it, or make a man more incapable of defending it, than intemperate heat and passion, whereby he injures and betrays the cause he is over anxious to maintain. "The wrath of man worketh not the righteousness of God," James i, 20.

Self-knowledge heals our animosities, and greatly cools our debates about matters of dark and doubtful speculation. One who knows himself sets too great a value upon his time and temper, to plunge rashly into those vain and fruitless controversies, in which one of them is sure to be lost, and the other in great danger of being so, especially when a man of bad temper and bad principles is the opponent; who aims rather to silence his adversary with overbearing confidence, dark unmeaning language, authoritative airs, and hard words, than convince him with solid argument; and who plainly contends, not for truth, but for victory. Little good can be done to the best cause in such a circumstance. And a wise and moderate man, who knows human nature, and knows himself, will rather give his antagonist the pleasure of an imaginary triumph, than engage in so unequal a combat.

An eagerness and zeal for dispute on every subject, and with every one, shows great self-sufficiency, that never-failing sign of great self-ignorance. And true moderation, which consists in an indifference about little things, and in a prudent and well-proportioned zeal about things of importance, can proceed from nothing but true knowledge, which has its foundation in self-acquaintance.

CHAPTER VI.

Self-knowledge improves the judgment.

VI. "ANOTHER great advantage of being well acquainted with ourselves is, that it helps us to form a better judgment of other things."

Self-knowledge, indeed, does not enlarge or increase our natural capacities, but it guides and regulates them; leads us to the right use and application of them; and removes a great many things which obstruct the due exercise of them, as pride, prejudice, and passion, &c., which oftentimes so miserably pervert the rational powers.

He that hath taken a just measure of himself, is thereby better able to judge of other things.

(1.) He knows how to judge of men and human nature better. For human nature, setting aside the difference of natural genius, and the improvements of education and religion, is pretty much the same in all. There are the same passions and appetites, the same natural infirmities and inclinations in all, though some are more predominant and distinguishable in some than they are in others. So that, if a man be but well acquainted with his own, this, together with a very little observation on the ways of men, will soon discover to him those of others, and show him very impartially the particular failings and excellences of men, and help him to form a much truer sentiment of them, than if he were to judge only by their exterior, the appearance they make in the eye of the world, (than which sometimes nothing shows them in a falser light,) or by popular opinions and prejudices.

(2.) Self-knowledge will teach us to judge rightly of facts as well as men. It will exhibit things to the mind in their proper light and true colours, without those false glasses and appearances which fancy throws upon them, or in which the imagination often paints them. It will teach us to judge, not with the imagination, but with the understanding; and will set a guard upon the former, which so often represents things in wrong views, and gives the mind false impressions of them. See part i, chapter iv.

(3.) It helps us to estimate the true value of all worldly good things. It rectifies our notions of them, and lessens that enormous esteem we are apt to have for them. For when a man knows himself, and his true interests, he will see how far, and in what degree, these things are suitable to him, and subservient to his good; and how far they are unsuitable, ensnaring, and pernicious. This, and not the common opinion of the world, will be his rule of judging concerning them. By this he will see quite through them; see what they really are at bottom, and how far a wise man ought to desire them. The reason why men value them so extravagantly is, because they take a superficial view of them, and only look upon their outside, where they are most showy and inviting. Were they to look within them, consider their intrinsic worth, their ordinary effects, their tendency, and their end, they would not be so apt to overvalue them. And a man that has learned to see through himself can easily see through these.*

CHAPTER VII.

Self-knowledge directs to the proper exercise of self-denial.

VII. "A MAN that knows himself, best knows how, and wherein, he ought to deny himself."

The great duty of self-denial, which our Saviour so expressly requires of all his followers, (plain and necessary as it is,) has been much mistaken and abused, and that not only by the Church of Rome, in their doctrines of penance, fasts, and pilgrimages, but by some Protestant Christians, in the instances of voluntary abstinence, and unnecessary austerities; whence they are sometimes apt to be too censorious

* "Riches, honours, powers, and the like, which owe all their worth to our false opinion of them, are too apt to draw the heart from virtue. We know not how to prize them; they are not to be judged of by the common report, but by their own nature. They have nothing to attract our esteem, but that we are used to admire them; they are not praised because they are things that ought to be desired, but they are desired because they are generally praised."—*Seneca.*

against those who indulge themselves in the use of those indifferent things, which they make it a point of conscience to abstain from. Whereas, would they confine their exercise of self-denial to the plain and important points of Christian practice, devoutly performing the necessary duties they are most averse to, and resolutely avoiding the known sins they are most inclined to, under the direction of Scripture, they would soon become more solid, judicious, and exemplary Christians: and did they know themselves, they would easily see, that herein there is occasion and scope enough for self-denial, and that to a degree of greater severity and difficulty than there is in those little corporeal abstinences and mortifications they enjoin themselves.

(1.) Self-knowledge will direct us to the necessary exercises of self-denial, with regard to the duties our tempers are most averse to.

There is no one, but, at some times, finds a great backwardness and indisposition to some duties, which he knows to be seasonable and necessary. This, then, is a proper occasion for self-discipline. For, to indulge this indisposition is very dangerous, and leads to an habitual neglect of known duty; and to resist and oppose it, and prepare for a diligent and faithful discharge of the duty, notwithstanding the many pleas and excuses that carnal disposition may urge for the neglect of it, this requires no small pains and self-denial, and yet is very necessary to the peace of conscience.

And, for our encouragement to this piece of self-denial, we need only remember, that the difficulty of the duty, or our unfitness for it, will, upon the trial, be found to be much less than we apprehended; and the pleasure of reflecting, that we have discharged our consciences, and given a fresh testimony of our uprightness, will more than compensate the pains and difficulty we found therein. And the oftener these criminal propensions to the wilful neglect of duty are opposed and overcome, the seldomer will they return, or the weaker will they grow, till at last, by divine grace, they will be wholly vanquished, and, in the room of them, will succeed an habitual "readiness to every good work," (Titus iii, 1,) and a very sensible delight therein; a much happier effect than can be expected from the severest exercises of self-denial in the instances before mentioned.

(2.) A man that knows himself, will see an equal necessity for self-denial, in order to check and control his inclinations to sinful actions; to subdue the rebel within; to resist the solicitations of sense and appetite; to summon all his wisdom to avoid the occasions and temptations to sin, and all his strength to oppose it.

All this (especially if it be a favourite or a constitutional inquiry) will cost a man pains and mortification enough; for instance, the subduing a violent passion, or taming a sensual inclination, or forgiving an apparent injury and affront. It is evident such a self-conquest can never be attained without much self-knowledge and self-denial.

And that self-denial that is exercised this way, as it will be a better evidence of our sincerity, so it will be more helpful and ornamental to the interests of religion, than the greatest zeal in those particular duties which are more suitable to our natural tempers, or than the greatest austerities in some particular instances of mortification, which are not so necessary, and perhaps not so difficult or disagreeable to us as this.

To what amazing heights of piety may some be thought to mount, (raised on the wings of a flaming zeal, and distinguished by uncommon preciseness and severity about little things,) who all the while, perhaps, cannot govern one passion, and appear yet ignorant of, and slaves to, their darling iniquity! Through an ignorance of themselves, they misapply their zeal, and misplace their self-denial, and, by that means, blemish their characters with a visible inconsistency.

CHAPTER VIII.

Self-knowledge promotes our usefulness in the world.

VIII. "The more we know of ourselves, the more useful we are like to be in those stations of life in which Providence hath fixed us."

When we know our proper talents and capacities, we know in what manner we are capable of being useful; and the consideration of our characters and relations in life will direct us to the proper application of those talents; show us to what ends they were given us, and to what purposes they ought to be cultivated and improved.

It is a sad thing to observe, how miserably some men debase and prostitute their capacities. Those gifts and indulgences of nature by which they outshine many others, and by which they are capable of doing real service to the cause of virtue and religion, and of being eminently useful to mankind, they either entirely neglect, or shamefully abuse, to the dishonour of God, and the prejudice of their fellow-creatures, by encouraging and imboldening them in the ways of vice and vanity. For the false glare of a profane wit will sometimes make such strong impressions on a weak, unsettled mind, as to overbear the principles of reason and wisdom, and give it too favourable sentiments of what it before abhorred; whereas the same force and sprightliness of genius would have been very happily and usefully employed in putting sin out of countenance, and in rallying the follies, and exposing the inconsistencies, of a vicious and profligate character.

When a man once knows where his strength lies, wherein he excels, or is capable of excelling, how far his influence extends, and in what station of life Providence hath fixed him, and the duties of that station, he then knows what talents he ought to cultivate, in what manner, and to what objects they are to be particularly directed and applied, in order to shine in that station, and be useful in it. This will keep him even and steady in his pursuits and views, consistent with himself, uniform in his conduct, and useful to mankind; and will prevent his shooting at a wrong mark, or missing the right mark he aims at, as thousands do for want of this necessary branch of self-knowledge.—See part i, chap. v.

CHAPTER IX.

Self-knowledge leads to a decorum and consistency of character.

IX. "A MAN that knows himself, knows how to act with discretion and dignity in every station and character."

Almost all the ridicule we see in the world takes its rise from self-ignorance; and to this, mankind, by common assent, ascribe it, when they say of a person that acts out of character, he does not know himself. Affectation is the spring of all ridicule, and self-ignorance the true source of affectation. A man that does not know his proper character, nor what becomes it, cannot act suitably to it. He will often affect a character which does not belong to him; and will either act above or beneath himself, which will make him equally contemptible in the eyes of them that know him.

A man of superior rank and character, that knows himself, knows that he is but a man;

subject to the same sicknesses, frailties, disappointments, pains, passions, and sorrows, as other men; that true honour lies in those things in which it is possible for the meanest peasant to exceed him, and therefore he will not be vainly arrogant. He knows that they are only transitory and accidental things that set him above the rest of mankind; that he will soon be upon a level with them; and therefore learns to condescend: and there is a dignity in this condescension; it does not sink, but exalts his reputation and character.

A man of inferior rank that knows himself, knows how to be content, quiet, and thankful in his lower sphere. As he has not an extravagant veneration and esteem for those external things which raise one man's circumstances so much above another's, so he does not look upon himself as the worse or less valuable man for not having them; much less does he envy them that have them. As he has not their advantages, so neither has he their temptations; he is in that state of life which the great Arbiter and Disposer of all things hath allotted him, and he is satisfied: but as a deference is owing to external superiority, he knows how to pay a proper respect to those that are above him, without that abject and servile cringing which discovers an inordinate esteem for their condition. As he does not over-esteem them for those little accidental advantages in which they excel him, so neither does he over-value himself for those things in which he excels others.

Were hearers to know themselves, they would not take upon them to dictate to their preachers, or teach their ministers how to teach them; (which, as St. Austin observes, is the same thing as if a patient, when he sends for a physician, should prescribe to him what he would have him prescribe;) but if they happen to hear something not quite agreeable to their former sentiments, would betake themselves more diligently to the study of their Bibles, to know "whether those things were so," Acts xvii, 11.

And were ministers to know themselves, they would know the nature and duty of their office, and the wants and infirmities of their hearers, better than to domineer over their faith, or shoot over their heads, and seek their own popularity rather than their benefit; they would be more solicitous for their edification than their approbation; and, like a faithful physician, would earnestly intend and endeavour their good, though it be in a way they may not like; and rather risk their own characters with weak and captious men, than "withhold any thing that is needful for them," or be unfaithful to God and their own consciences. The most palatable food is not always the most wholesome. Patients must not expect to be always pleased, nor physicians to be always applauded.

CHAPTER X.

Piety the effect of self-knowledge.

X. "SELF-KNOWLEDGE tends greatly to cultivate a spirit of true piety."

Ignorance is so far from being the mother of devotion, that nothing is more destructive of it; and of all ignorance none is a greater bane to it than self-ignorance. This, indeed, is very consistent with superstition, bigotry, and enthusiasm, those common counterfeits of piety, which, by weak and credulous minds, are often mistaken for it. But true piety and real devotion can only spring from a just knowledge of God and ourselves; and the relation we stand in to him, and the dependance we have upon him. For when we consider ourselves as the creatures of God, whom he made for his honour; and as creatures incapable of any happiness but what results from his favour; and as entirely and continually dependant upon him for every thing we have and hope for; and while we bear this thought in our minds, what can induce or prompt us more to love, and to fear, and trust him, as our God, our Father, and all-sufficient Friend and Helper?

CHAPTER XI.

Self-knowledge teaches us rightly to perform the duties of religion.

XI. "SELF-KNOWLEDGE will be a good help and direction to us in many of our religious duties and Christian exercises." Particularly,

(1.) In the duty of prayer, both as to the matter and the mode. He that rightly knows himself will be very sensible of his spiritual wants, and he that is well acquainted with his spiritual wants will not be at a loss what to pray for. "Our hearts would be the best prayer-books, if we were skilful in reading them. Why do men pray, and call for prayers, when they come to die, but that they begin a little better to know themselves? And were they now but to hear the voice of God and conscience, they would not remain speechless. But they that are born deaf are always dumb."—*Baxter*.

Again, self-knowledge will teach us to pray, not only with fluency, but fervency ; will help us to keep the heart, as well as order our speech, before God ; and so promote the grace as well as gift of prayer. Did we but seriously consider what we are, and what we are about ; whom we pray to, and what we pray for ; it is impossible we should be so dead, spiritless, and formal in this duty as we too often are. The very thought would inspire us with life, and faith, and fervour.

(2.) Self-knowledge will be very helpful to us in the duty of thanksgiving : as it makes us mindful of the mercies we receive ; the suitableness and the seasonableness of them. A self-knowing man considers what he hath, as well as what he wants ; is at once sensible, both of the value of his mercies, and his unworthiness of them : and this is what makes him thankful. For this reason it is, that one Christian's heart even melts with gratitude for those very mercies which others disesteem and depreciate, and perhaps despise, because they have not what they think greater. But a man that knows himself, knows that he deserves nothing, and therefore is thankful for every thing. For thankfulness as necessarily flows from humility, as humility does from self-acquaintance.

(3.) In the duties of reading and hearing the word of God, self-knowledge is of excellent use, to enable us to understand and apply that which we read or hear. Did we understand our hearts better, we should understand the word of God better, for that speaks to the heart. A man that is acquainted with his heart, easily sees how it penetrates and explores, searches and lays open its most inward parts. He feels what he reads ; and finds that a quickening spirit, which, to a self-ignorant man, is but a dead letter.

Moreover, this self-acquaintance teaches a man to apply what he reads and hears of the word of God ; he sees the pertinence, congruity, and suitableness of it to his own case ; and lays it up faithfully in the store-room of his mind, to be digested and improved by his after thoughts. And it is by this art of aptly applying Scripture, and urging the most suitable instructions and admonitions of it home upon our consciences, that we receive the greatest benefit by it.

(4.) Nothing is of more eminent service in the great duty of meditation, especially in that part of it which consists in heart converse. A man who is unacquainted with himself, is as unfit to converse with his heart as he is with a stranger he never saw, and whose taste and temper he is altogether unacquainted with: he knows not how to get his thoughts about him; and when he has, he knows not how to range and fix them, and hath no more the command of them, than a general has of a wild, undisciplined army, that has never been exercised, or accustomed to obedience and order. But one, who hath made it the study of his life to be acquainted with himself, is soon disposed to enter into a free and familiar converse with his own heart; and in such a self-conference improves more in true wisdom, and acquires more useful and substantial knowledge, than he could do from the most polite and refined conversation in the world. Of such excellent use is self-knowledge in all the duties of piety and devotion.

CHAPTER XII.

Self-knowledge the best preparation for death.

XII. " SELF-KNOWLEDGE will be an habitual preparation for death, and a constant guard against the surprise of it," because it fixes and settles our hopes of future happiness. That which makes the thoughts of death so terrifying to the soul, is its utter uncertainty what will become of it after death. Were this uncertainty but removed, a thousand things would reconcile us to the thoughts of dying.*

"Distrust and darkness of a future state
Is that which makes mankind to dread their fate:
Dying is nothing; but 'tis this we fear,
To be we know not what, we know not where."

Now, self-knowledge, in a good degree, removes this uncertainty: for, as the word of God hath revealed the certainty of a future state of happiness, which good men shall enter upon after death, and plainly described the requisite qualifications for it; when a good man,

* It is this makes us averse from death, that it translates us to things we are unacquainted with, and we tremble at the thought of those things that are unknown to us. We are naturally afraid of being in the dark; and death is a leap in the dark.

by a long and laborious self-acquaintance, comes distinctly to discern those qualifications in himself, his hopes of heaven soon raise him above the fears of death ; and though he may not be able to form any clear or distinct conception of the nature of that happiness, yet, in general, he is assured, that it will be a most exquisite and satisfying one, and will contain in it every thing necessary to make it complete, because it will come immediately from God himself. Whereas, they who are ignorant what they are, must necessarily be ignorant what they shall be. A man that is all darkness within, can have but a dark prospect forward.*

O ! what would we not give for solid hope in death ! Reader, wouldst thou have it, know God, and know thyself.

* Who exposed to others eyes
Into his own heart never pries,
Death's to him a strange surprise.

A TREATISE

ON

SELF-KNOWLEDGE.

PART III.

Showing how self-knowledge is to be attained.

FROM what hath been said under the two former parts of the subject, self-knowledge appears to be in itself so excellent, and its effects so extensively useful and conducive to the happiness of human kind, that nothing need further be added by way of motive or inducement to excite us to make it the great object of our study and pursuit. If we regard our present peace, satisfaction, and usefulness, or our future and everlasting interests, we shall certainly value and prosecute this knowledge above all others, as what will be most ornamental to our characters, and beneficial to our interest, in every state of life, and abundantly recompense all our labour.

Were there need of any further motives to excite us to this, I might lay open the many dreadful effects of self-ignorance, and show how plainly it appears to be the original spring of all the follies and incongruities we see in the characters of men, and of most of the mortifications and miseries they meet with here. This would soon appear, by only mentioning the reverse of those advantages before specified, which naturally attend self-knowledge : for what is it but a want of self-knowledge and self-government that makes us so unsettled and volatile in our dispositions ? so subject to transport and excess of passions in the varying scenes of life ? so rash and unguarded in our conduct ? so vain and self-sufficient ? so censorious and malignant ? so eager and confident ? so little useful in the world to what we might be ? so inconsistent with ourselves ? so mistaken in our notions of true religion ? so generally indisposed to, or unengaged in, the holy exercises of it ? and, finally, so unfit for death, and so afraid of dying ? I say, to what is all this owing, but self-ignorance ? the first and fruitful source of all this long train of evils. And, indeed, there is scarce any but what may be traced up to it. In short, it brutifies man to be ignorant of himself. " Man that is in honour, and understandeth not, (himself especially,) is as the beasts that perish," Psalm xlix, 20.

"Come home, then, O my wandering, self-neglecting soul! lose not thyself in a wilderness or tumult of impertinent, vain, distracting things. Thy work is nearer thee: the country thou shouldst first survey and travel is within thee; from which thou must pass to that above thee; when, by losing thyself in this without thee, thou wilt find thyself, before thou art aware, in that below thee. Let the eyes of fools be in the corners of the earth; leave it to men beside themselves to live as without themselves; do thou keep at home, and mind thine own business; survey thyself, thine own make and nature, and thou wilt find full employ for all thy most active thoughts. But, dost thou delight in the mysteries of nature? consider well the mystery of thy own. The compendium of all thou studiest is near thee, even within thee; thyself being the epitome of the world.* If either necessity or duty, nature or grace, reason or faith, internal inducements, external impulses, or eternal motives, might

* Who can sufficiently admire the noble nature of that creature man, who hath in him the mortal and the immortal, the rational and the irrational natures united, and so carries about with him the image of the whole creation? whence he is called microcosm, or the little world.

determine the subject of thy study and c' plation, thou wouldst call home thy distracted thoughts, and employ them more on thyself and thy God."—*Baxter's Mischief of Self-ignorance.*

Now, then, let us resolve, that henceforth the study of ourselves shall be the business of our lives; that, by the blessing of God, we may arrive at such a degree of self-knowledge as may secure to us the excellent benefits before mentioned: to which end we would do well to attend diligently to the rules laid down in the following chapters.

CHAPTER I.

Self-examination necessary to self-knowledge.

I. "THE first thing necessary to self-knowledge is self-inspection."

We must often look into our hearts, if we would know them. They are very deceitful; more so than any man can think, till he has searched, and tried, and watched them. We may meet with frauds and faithless dealings from men; but, after all, our own hearts are the greatest cheats, and there are none we are in greater danger from than ourselves. We must first suspect ourselves, then examine ourselves, then watch ourselves, if we expect ever to know ourselves. How is it possible there should be any self-acquaintance without self-converse?

Were a man to accustom himself to such self-employment, he need not live "till thirty, before he suspects himself a fool, or till forty, before he knows it."*—*Night Thoughts*, part i.

Men could never be so bad as they are if they did but take a proper care and scope in this business of self-examination; if they did but look backward to what they were, inward to what they are, and forward to what they shall be.

And as this is the first and most necessary step to self-acquaintance, it may not be amiss to be a little more particular in it. Therefore,

(1.) This business of self-scrutiny must be performed with great care and diligence, otherwise our hearts will deceive us even while we are examining them. "When we set ourselves

* "At thirty man suspects himself a fool,
Knows it at forty, and reforms his plan;
At fifty chides his infamous delay,
Pushes his prudent purpose to *resolve;*
In all the magnanimity of thought
Resolves, and re-resolves; then dies the same."
Night Thoughts.

to think, some trifle or other presently interrupts and draws us off from any profitable recollection. Nay, we ourselves fly out, and are glad to be diverted from a severe examination into our own state; which is sure, if diligently pursued, to present us with objects of shame and sorrow, which will wound our sight, and soon make us weary of this necessary work."—*Stanhope's Thomas à Kempis*, p. 166.

Do not let us flatter ourselves, then, that this is a mighty easy business: much pains and care are necessary sometimes to keep the mind intent, and more to keep it impartial; and the difficulty of it is the reason that so many are averse to it, and care not to descend into themselves.

Reader, try the experiment; retire now into thyself, and see if thou canst not strike out some light within, by closely urging such questions as these:—"What am I? for what was I made? and to what ends have I been preserved so long by the favour of my Maker? Do I remember, or forget those ends? Have I answered, or perverted them? What have I been doing since I came into the world? What is the world or myself the better for my living so many years in it? What is my allowed course of actions? Am I sure it will bear the future test? Am I now in that state I shall wish to die in? And, O my soul, think, and think again, what it is to die! Do not put that most awful event far from thee; nor pass it by with a superficial thought. Canst thou be too well fortified against the terrors of that day? and art thou sure that the props which support thee now will not fail thee then? What hopes hast thou for eternity? Hast thou, indeed, that holy, godlike temper, which alone can fit thee for the enjoyment of God? Which world art thou most concerned for? What things do most deeply affect thee? O my soul, remember thy dignity; think how soon the scene will shift. Why shouldest thou forget thou art immortal?"

(2.) This self-excitation and scrutiny must be very frequently made. They who have a great deal of important business on their hands should be often looking over their accounts, and frequently adjustiny them, lest they should be going backward, and not know it; and custom will soon take off the difficulty of this duty, and turn it into delight.

In our morning retreat, it will be proper to remember that we cannot preserve throughout the day that calm and even temper we may then be in; that we shall very probably meet with some things to ruffle us, some attack on our weak side. Place a guard there now. Or, however, if no incidents happen to discompose us, our tempers will vary; our thoughts will flow pretty much with our blood; and the dispositions of the mind be a good deal governed by the motions of the animal spirits; our souls will be serene or cloudy, our tempers volatile or phlegmatic, and our inclinations sober or irregular, according to the briskness or sluggishness of the circulation of the animal fluids, whatever may be the cause or immediate occasion of that, and therefore we must resolve to avoid all occasions that may raise any dangerous ferments there, which, when once raised, will excite in us very different thoughts and dispositions from those we now have; which, together with the force of a fair opportunity and urgent temptation, may overset our reason and resolution, and betray us into those sinful indulgences which will wound the conscience, stain the soul, and create bitter remorse in our cooler reflections. Pious thoughts and purposes, in the morning, will set a guard upon the soul, and fortify it under all the temptations of the day.

But such self-inspection, however, should never fail to make part of our evening devotions, when we should review and examine the several actions of the day, the various tempers and dispositions we have been in, and the occasions that excited them. It is an advice worthy of a Christian, though it first dropped from a heathen pen, that, before we betake ourselves to rest, we review and examine all the passages of the day, that we may have the comfort of what we have done aright, and may redress what we find to have been amiss; and make the shipwrecks of one day be as marks to direct our course on another; a practice that hath been recommended by many of the heathen moralists of the greatest name, as Plutarch, Epictetus, Marcus Antoninus; and particularly Pythagoras, in the verses that go under his name, and are called his golden verses;* wherein he advises his scholars every night to recollect the passages of the day, and ask themselves these questions: "Wherein have I trans-

* "Let not the stealing god of sleep surprise
Nor creep in slumbers on thy weary eyes,
Ere ev'ry action of the former day
Strictly thou dost, and righteously survey.
With rev'rence at thy own tribunal stand,
And answer justly to thy own demand.
Where have I been? In what have I transgress'd?
What good or ill has this day's life express'd?
Where have I fail'd in what I ought to do?
In what to God, to man, or to myself, I owe?
Inquire severe whate'er from first to last,
From morning's dawn 'till evening's gloom has past.

gressed this day? what have I done? what duty have I omitted?" &c. Seneca recommends the same practice. "Sectius," saith he, "did this: at the close of the day, before he betook himself to rest, he addressed his soul in the following manner,—What evil of thine hast thou cured this day? what vice withstood? in what respect art thou better? Passion will cease, or become more cool, when it knows it is every day to be thus called to account. What can be more advantageous than this constant custom of searching through the day?—And the same course," saith Seneca, "I take myself; and every day sit in judgment on myself. And at even, when all is hush and still, I make a scrutiny into the day; look over my words and actions, and hide nothing from myself; conceal none of my mistakes through fear. For why should I, when I have it in my power to say thus?—This once I forgive thee, but see thou do so no more. In such a dispute I was too keen: do not, for the future, contend with ignorant men; they will not be

---

If evil were thy deeds, repenting mourn,
And let thy soul with strong remorse be torn.
If good, the good with peace of mind repay,
And to thy secret self with pleasure say,
Rejoice, my heart, for all went well to-day."

convinced, because they are unwilling to show their ignorance. Such a one I reproved with too much freedom, whereby I have not reformed, but exasperated him: remember hereafter to be more mild in your censures; and consider not only whether what you say be true, but whether the person you say it to can bear to hear the truth."—*Seneca, de Ira.*, lib. iii, cap. 36. Thus far that excellent moralist.

Let us take a few other specimens of a more pious and Christian turn, from a judicious and devout writer.

"This morning when I arose, instead of applying myself to God in prayer, (which I generally find it best to do immediately after a few serious reflections,) I gave way to idle musing, to the great disorder of my heart and frame. How often have I suffered for want of more watchfulness on this occasion! When shall I be wise? I have this day shamefully trifled almost through the whole of it; was in my bed when I should have been upon my knees; prayed but coolly in the morning; was strangely off my guard in the business and conversation I was concerned with in the day, particularly at ——; I indulged to very foolish, sinful, vile thoughts, &c. I fell in with a strain of conversation too common among all sorts, namely, speaking evil of others; taking up a reproach against my neighbour. I have often resolved against this sin, and yet run into it again. How treacherous this wicked heart of mine! I have lost several hours this day in mere sauntering and idleness. This day I had an instance of mine own infirmity, that I was a little surprised at, and I am sure I ought to be humbled for. The behaviour of ——, from whom I can expect nothing but humour, indiscretion, and folly, strangely ruffled me; and that after I have had warning over and over again. What a poor, impotent, contemptible creature am I! This day I have been kept, in a great measure, from my too frequent failings. I had this day very comfortable assistances from God, upon an occasion not a littly trying—what shall I render?" —*Bennet's Christ. Orat.*

(3.) See that the mind be in the most composed and disengaged frame it can, when you enter upon this business of self-judgment. Choose a time when it is most free from passion, and most at leisure from the cares and affairs of life. A judge is not like to bring a cause to a good issue, that is either intoxicated with liquor on the bench, or has his mind distracted with other cares, when he should be intent on the trial. Remember you sit in judgment upon yourself, and have nothing to do at present but to sift the evidence which conscience may bring in either for or against you, in order to pronounce a just sentence, which is of much greater concernment to you at present than any thing else can be; and therefore it should be transacted with the utmost care, composure, and attention.

(4.) Beware of partiality, and the influence of self-love, in this weighty business; which, if you do not guard against it, will soon lead you into self-delusion, the consequences of which may be fatal to you. Labour to see yourself as you are; and view things in the light in which they are, and not in that in which you would have them be. Remember, that the mind is always apt to believe those things true, which it would have be so; and backward to believe those things true, which it wishes were not so; and this is an influence you will certainly lie under in this affair of self-judgment.

You need not be much afraid of being too severe upon yourself; your great danger will generally be, passing a too favourable judgment. A judge ought not, indeed, to be a party concerned, and should have no interest in the person he sits in judgment upon. But this cannot be the case here, as you yourself are both judge and criminal, which shows the danger of pronouncing a too favourable sentence. But remember your business is only with the evidence and the rule of judgment; and that, however you come off now, there will be a rehearing in another court, where judgment will be according to truth.

" However, look not unequally, either at the good or evil that is in you, but view them as they are. If you observe only the good that is in you, and overlook the bad, or search only after your faults, and overlook your graces, neither of these will bring you to a true acquaintance with yourself."—*Baxter's Director.*

And to induce you to this impartiality, remember that this business (though it may be hid from the world) is not done in secret. God sees how you manage it, before whose tribunal you must expect a righteous judgment. "We should order our thoughts so," saith Seneca, "as if we had a window in our breasts, through which any one might see what passes there. And indeed there is one that does; for what does it signify that our thoughts are hid from men? From God nothing is hid."—*Seneca's Epist.* 84.

(5.) Beware of false rules of judgment. This is a sure and common way to self-deception.

For example: Some judge themselves by what they have been. But it does not follow, if men are not so bad as they have been, that therefore they are as good as they should be. It is wrong to make our past conduct implicitly the measure of our present; or our present the rule of our future; when our past, present, and future conduct must all be brought to another rule. And they who thus "measure themselves by themselves, and compare themselves with themselves, are not wise," 2 Cor. x, 12. Again, others are apt to judge of themselves by the opinions of men, which is the most uncertain rule that can be; for in that very opinion of theirs you may be deceived. How do you know they have really so good an opinion of you as they profess? but if they have, have not others as bad? and why should not the opinion of these be your rule as well as the opinion of those? Appeal to self-flattery for an answer. However, neither one nor the other of them, perhaps, appear to know themselves, and how should they know you? How is it possible they should have opportunities of knowing you better than you know yourself? A man can never gain a right knowledge of himself from the opinion of others, which is so various, and generally so ill-founded; for men commonly judge by outward appearances, or inward prejudice, and therefore, for the most part, think and speak of us very much at random. Again, others are for judging of themselves by the conduct of their superiors, who have opportunities and advantages of knowing, acting, and being better; and yet, without vanity be it spoken, say they, we are not behindhand with them. But what then? Neither they nor you, perhaps, are what the obligations of your character indispensably require you to be, and what you must be, ere you can be happy. But consider how easily this argument may be turned upon you: you are better than some, you say, who have greater opportunities and advantages of being good than you have, and therefore your state is safe; but you yourself have greater opportunities and advantages of being good than some others have, who are, nevertheless, better than you; and therefore, by the same rule, your state cannot be safe. Again, others judge of themselves by the common maxims of the vulgar world concerning honour and honesty, virtue and interest, which maxims, though generally very corrupt, and very contrary to those of reason, conscience, and Scripture, men will follow as a rule, for the sake of the latitude it allows them; and fondly think, that, if they stand right in the opinion of the lowest kind of men, they have no reason to be severe upon themselves. Others, whose sentiments are more delicate and refined, they imagine, may be mistaken, or may overstrain the matter. In which persuasion they are confirmed, by observing how seldom the consciences of the generality of men smite them for those things which these nice judges condemn as heinous crimes. I need not say how false and pernicious a rule this is. Again, others may judge of themselves and their state by sudden impressions they have had, or strong impulses upon their spirits, which they attribute to the finger of God; and by which they have been so exceedingly affected, as to make no doubt but that it was the instant of their conversion: but whether it was or not, can never be known but by the conduct of their after lives. In like manner, others judge of their good state by their good frames, though very rare it may be, and very transient, soon passing off "like a morning cloud, or as the early dew." "But we should not judge of ourselves by that which is unusual or extraordinary with us, but by the ordinary tenor and drift of our lives. A bad man may seem good in some good mood, and a good man may seem bad in some extraordinary falls. To judge of a bad man by his best hours, and a good man by his worst, is the way to be deceived in them both."—*Baxter's Director.*

And the same way may you be deceived in yourself. Pharaoh, Ahab, Herod, and Felix, had all of them their softenings, their transitory fits of goodness; but yet they remain upon record under the blackest characters.

These, then, are all the wrong rules of judgment; and to trust to them, or try ourselves by them, leads to fatal self-deception. Again,

(6.) In the business of self-examination, you must not only take care you do not judge by wrong rules, but that you do not judge wrong by right rules. You must endeavour, then, to be well acquainted with them. The office of a judge is not only to collect the evidence and the circumstances of facts, but to be well skilled in the laws by which those facts are to be examined.

Now, the only right rules by which we are to examine, in order to know ourselves, are reason and Scripture. Some are for setting aside these rules, as too severe for them, too stiff to bend to their perverseness, too straight to measure their crooked ways; are against reason, when reason is against them; decrying it as carnal reason; and, for the same cause, are against Scripture too, depreciating it as a dead letter. And thus, rather than be convinced they are wrong, they despise the only means that can set them right.

And as some are for setting aside each part of their rules, so others are for setting them one against the other; reason against Scripture, and Scripture against reason; when they are both given us by the God of our natures, not only as perfectly consistent, but as proper to explain and illustrate each other, and prevent our mistaking either; and to be, when taken together, (as they always should,) the most complete and only rule by which to judge both of ourselves, and every thing belonging to our salvation, as reasonable and fallen creatures.

(1.) Then, one part of that rule, which God hath given us to judge of ourselves by, is right reason: by which I do not mean the reasoning of any particular man, which may be very different from the reasoning of another particular man, and both, it may be, very different from right reason; because both may be influenced, not so much by the reason and nature of things, as by partial prepossessions and the power of passions: but, by right reason I mean those common principles which are readily allowed by all who are capable of understanding them, and not notoriously perverted by the power of prejudice, and which are confirmed by the common consent of all the sober and thinking part of mankind, and may be easily learned by the light of nature. Therefore, if any doctrine or practice, though supposed to be founded in, or countenanced by, revelation, be nevertheless apparently repugnant to these dictates of right reason, or evidently contradict our natural notions of the divine attributes, or weaken our obligations to universal virtue, that, we may be sure, is no part of revelation, because then one part of our rule would clash with, and be opposite to, the other. And thus reason was designed to be our guard against a wild and extravagant construction of Scripture.

(2.) The other part of our rule is the sacred Scriptures, which we are to use as our guard against the licentious excursions of fancy, which is often imposing itself upon us for right reason. Let any religious scheme or notion, then, appear ever so pleasing or plausible, if it be not established on the plain principles of Scripture, it is forthwith to be discarded; and that sense of Scripture that is violently forced to bend toward it, is very much to be suspected.

It must be very surprising to one who reads

and studies the sacred Scriptures with a free unbiased mind, to see what elaborate, fine-spun, and flimsy glosses men will invent and put upon some texts as the true and genuine sense of them, for no other reason, but because it is most agreeable to the opinion of their party, from which, as the standard of their orthodoxy, they durst never depart; who, if they were to write a critique, in the same manner, on any Greek or Latin author, would make themselves extremely ridiculous in the eyes of the learned world. But, if we would not pervert our rule, we must learn to think as Scripture speaks, and not compel that to speak as we think. Would we know ourselves, then, we must often view ourselves in the glass of God's word; and when we have taken a full survey of ourselves from thence, let us not soon forget "what manner of persons we are," James i, 23, 24. If our own image do not please us, let us not quarrel with our mirror, but set about mending ourselves.

The eye of the mind, indeed, is not like that of the body, which can see every thing else but itself; for the eye of the mind can turn itself inward, and survey itself. However, it must be owned, it can see itself much better when its own image is reflected upon it from this mirror. And it is by this only that we can come at the bottom of our hearts, and discover those secret prejudices and carnal prepossessions which self-love would hide from us.

This, then, is the first thing we must do in order to self-knowledge. We must examine, scrutinize, and judge ourselves diligently, leisurely, frequently, and impartially; and that not by the false maxims of the world, but by the rules which God hath given us, reason and Scripture; and take care to understand those rules, and not set them at variance. The next important step to self-knowledge is the subject of the following chapter.

CHAPTER II.

Constant watchfulness necessary to self-knowledge.

II. "WOULD we know ourselves, we must be very watchful over our hearts and lives."

(1.) We must keep a vigilant eye upon our hearts, that is, our tempers, inclinations, and passions. A more necessary piece of advice we cannot practise, in order to self-acquaintance, than that which Solomon gives us, Prov. iv, 23, "Keep your heart with all diligence," or, as it is in the original, "above all keeping." As if it were said, Whatever you neglect or overlook, be sure you mind your heart.* Narrowly observe all its inclinations and aversions, all its motions and affections, together with the several objects and occasions which excite them. And this precept is enforced with two very urgent reasons in Scripture. The first is, because "out of it are the issues of life." That is, as our heart is, so will the tenor of our life and conduct be. As is the fountain, so are the streams; as is the root, so is the fruit. Matt. vii, 18. And the other is, because "it is deceitful above all things," Jer. xvii, 9. And, therefore, without a constant guard upon it, we shall insensibly run into many hurtful self-deceptions. To which I may add, that, without this careful keeping of the heart, we shall never be able to acquire any considerable degree of self-acquaintance or self-government.

(2.) To know ourselves, we must watch our life and conduct, as well as our hearts: and, by this, the heart will be better known; as the root is best known by the fruit. We must attend to the nature and consequences of every action we are disposed or solicited to, before

* Parallel to this advice of the royal preacher is that of M. Aurelius: "Look within; for within is the fountain of good."

we comply; and consider how it will appear in an impartial review. We are apt enough to observe and watch the conduct of others; a wise man will be as critical and as severe upon his own: for indeed we have a great deal more to do with our own conduct than other men's; as we are to answer for our own, but not for theirs. By observing the conduct of other men, we know them; by carefully observing our own, we must know ourselves.

CHAPTER III.

We should have some regard to the opinions of others concerning us, particularly of our enemies.

III. "WOULD we know ourselves, we should not altogether neglect the opinion which others have of us, or the things they may say of us."

Not that we need be very solicitous about the censure or applause of the world, which is generally very rash and wrong, according to the particular humours and prepossessions of men; and a man that knows himself will soon know how to despise them both. "The judgment which the world makes of us, is generally of no manner of use to us; it adds nothing to our souls or bodies, nor lessens any of our miseries.

Let us constantly follow reason," says Montaigne, "and let the public approbation follow us the same way if it pleases."

But still, I say, a total indifference in this matter is unwise. We ought not to be entirely insensible to the reports of others; no, not to the railings of an enemy; for an enemy may say something out of ill-will to us, which it may concern us to think of coolly when we are by ourselves; to examine whether the accusation be just, and what there is in our conduct and temper which may make it appear so. And by this means our enemy may do us more good than he intended, and be an occasion of discovering something of our hearts to us, which we did not know before. A man that hath no enemies, ought to have very faithful friends; and one who hath no such friends, ought to think it no calamity that he hath enemies to be his effectual monitors. "Our friends," says Mr. Addison, "very often flatter us as much as our own hearts. They either do not see our faults, or conceal them from us; or soften them by their representations, after such a manner, that we think them too trivial to be taken notice of. An adversary, on the contrary, makes a stricter search into us, discovers every flaw and imperfection in our tempers; and, though his malice may set them in too strong a light, it has generally some ground for what it advances. A friend exaggerates a man's virtues; an enemy inflames his crimes. A wise man should give a just attention to both of them, so far as it may tend to the improvement of the one, and the diminution of the other. Plutarch has written an essay on the benefits which a man may receive from his enemies; and among the good fruits of enmity, mentions this in particular, that, by the reproaches it casts upon us, we see the worst side of ourselves, and open our eyes to several blemishes and defects in our lives and conversations, which we should not have observed without the help of such ill-natured monitors.

"In order, likewise, to come at a true knowledge of ourselves, we should consider, on the other hand, how far we may deserve the praises and approbation which the world bestow upon us; whether the actions they celebrate proceed from laudable and worthy motives, and how far we are really possessed of the virtues which gain us applause among those with whom we converse. Such a reflection is absolutely necessary, if we consider how apt we are either to value or condemn ourselves by the opinions of others, and to sacrifice the report of our own hearts to the judgment of the world."*—*Spectator*, vol. vi, No. 399.

* In that treatise of Plutarch, here referred to, there are a great many excellent things pertinent to this subject; and therefore I thought it not improper to throw a few extracts out of it into the margin.

"The foolish and inconsiderate spoil the very friendships they are engaged in; but the wise and prudent make good use of the hatred and enmity of men against them.

"Why should we not take an enemy for our tutor, who will instruct us gratis in those things we knew not before? For an enemy sees and understands more in matters relating to us than our friends do. Because love is blind; but spite, malice, ill-will, wrath, and contempt talk much, are very inquisitive and quick-sighted.

"Our enemy, to gratify his ill-will toward us, acquaints himself with the infirmities both of our bodies and minds; sticks to our faults, and makes his invidious remarks upon them, and spreads them abroad by his uncharitable and ill-natured reports. Hence we are taught this useful lesson for the direction and management of our conversation in the world, namely, that we be circumspect and wary in every thing we speak or do, as if our enemy always stood at our elbow, and overlooked our actions.

"Those persons whom that wisdom hath brought to live soberly, which the fear and awe of enemies hath infused, are by degrees drawn into a habit of living so, and are composed and fixed in their obedience to virtue by custom and use.

"When Diogenes was asked how he might be avenged of his enemies, he replied, To be yourself a good and honest man.

"Antisthenes spake incomparably well; 'that if a man would live a safe and unblameable life, it was necessary that he should have very ingenuous and faithful friends, or very bad enemies; because the first by their kind admonitions would keep him from sinning, the latter by their invectives.'

It is the character of a very dissolute mind, to be entirely insensible to all that the world says of us; and shows such a confidence of

"He that hath no friend to give him advice or reprove him when he does amiss, must bear patiently the rebukes of his enemies, and thereby learn to mend the errors of his ways; and consider seriously the object which these severe censures aim at, and not what he is who makes them. For he who designed the death of Promotheus the Thessalian, instead of giving him a fatal blow, only opened a swelling which he had, which did really save his life. Just so may the harsh reprehensions of enemies cure some distempers of the mind, which were before either not known or neglected; though their angry speeches do originally proceed from malice or ill-will.

"If any man with opprobrious language objects to you crimes you know nothing of, you ought to inquire into the causes or reasons of such false accusations; whereby you may learn to take heed for the future, lest you should unwarily commit those offences which are unjustly imputed to you.

"Whenever any thing is spoken against you that is not true, do not pass it by, nor despise it because it is false; but forthwith examine yourself, and consider what you have said or done that may administer a just occasion of reproof.

"Nothing can be a greater instance of wisdom and humanity, than for a man to bear silently and quietly the follies and revilings of an enemy; taking as much care not to provoke him, as he would to sail safely by a dangerous rock.

"It is an eminent piece of humanity, and a manifest token of a nature generally generous, to put up with the affronts of an enemy at a time when you have a fair opportunity to revenge them.

"Let us carefully observe those good qualities wherein our enemies excel us; and endeavour to excel them, by avoiding what is faulty, and imitating what is excellent in them."

self-knowledge, as is usually a sure sign of self-ignorance. The most knowing minds are ever least presumptuous. And true self-knowledge is a science of so much depth and difficulty, that a wise man would not choose to be over confident that all his notions of himself are right, in opposition to the judgment of all mankind ; some of whom, perhaps, have better opportunities and advantages of knowing him (at some seasons especially) than he has of knowing himself ; because they never look through the same false medium of self-flattery.

CHAPTER IV.

Frequent converse with superiors a help to self-knowledge.

IV. "Another proper means of self-knowledge is to converse as much as you can with those who are your superiors in real excellence."

"He that walketh with wise men, shall be wise," Prov. xiii, 20. Their example will not only be your motive to laudable pursuits, but a mirror to your mind, by which you may possibly discern some failings, or deficiencies, or neglects, in yourself, which before escaped you.

You will see the unreasonableness of your vanity and self-sufficiency, when you observe how much you are surpassed by others in knowledge and goodness. Their proficiency will make your defects the more obvious to you. And, by the lustre of their virtues, you will better see the deformity of your vices; your negligence by their diligence; your pride by their humility; your passion by their meekness; and your folly by their wisdom.

Examples not only move, but teach and direct much more effectually than precepts; and show us, not only that such virtues may be practised, but how; and how lovely they appear when they are. And, therefore, if we cannot have them always before our eyes, we should endeavour to have them always in our mind; and especially that of our great Head and Pattern, who hath set us a lovely example of the most innocent conduct, under the worst and most disadvantageous circumstances of human life.

CHAPTER V.

Of cultivating such a temper as will be the best disposition to self-knowledge.

V. " If a man would know himself, he must, with great care, cultivate that temper which will best dispose him to receive this knowledge."

Now, as there are no greater hinderances to self-knowledge than pride and obstinacy, so there is nothing more helpful to it than humility and an openness to conviction.

(1.) One who is in quest of self-knowledge, must, above all things, seek humility. And how near an affinity there is between these two, appears from hence, that they are both acquired the same way. The very means of attaining humility are the properest means for attaining self-knowledge. By keeping an eye every day upon our faults and wants, we become more humble; and, by the same means, we become more self-knowing. By considering how far we fall short of our rule and our duty, and how vastly others exceed us, and especially by a daily and diligent study of the word of God, we come to have meaner thoughts of ourselves; and, by the very same means, we come to have a better acquaintance with ourselves.

A proud man cannot know himself. Pride is that beam in the eye of his mind which renders him quite blind to any blemishes there. Hence, nothing is a surer sign of self-ignorance than vanity and ostentation.

Indeed, true self-knowledge and humility are so necessarily connected, that they depend upon, and mutually beget, each other. A man that knows himself, knows the worst of himself, and therefore cannot but be humble; and an humble mind is frequently contemplating its own faults and weaknesses, which greatly improves it in self-knowledge. So that self-acquaintance makes a man humble; and humility gives him still a better acquaintance with himself.

(2.) An openness to conviction is no less necessary to self-knowledge than humility.

As nothing is a greater bar to true knowledge than an obstinate stiffness in opinion, and a fear to depart from old notions, which (before we were capable of judging perhaps) we had long taken up for the truth, so nothing is a greater bar to self-knowledge than a strong aversion to part with those sentiments of ourselves which we have been blindly accustomed to, and to think worse of ourselves than we are used.

And such an unwillingness to retract our sentiments, in both cases, proceeds from the same cause, namely, a reluctance to self-condemnation. For he that takes up a new way of thinking, contrary to that which he hath long received, therein condemns himself of having lived in an error; and he that begins to see faults in himself he never saw before, condemns himself of having lived in ignorance and sin. Now this is an ungrateful business, and what self-flattery gives us a strong aversion to.

But such an inflexibility of judgment, and hatred of conviction, is a very unhappy and hurtful turn of mind; and a man that is resolved never to be in the wrong, is in a fair way never to be in the right.

As infallibility is no privilege of the human nature, it is no diminution to a man's good sense or judgment to be found in an error, provided he is willing to retract it. He acts with the same freedom and liberty as before; whoever be his monitor, it is his own good sense and judgment that still guide him; which shine to great advantage in thus directing him against the bias of vanity and self-opinion. And in thus changing his sentiments, he only acknowledges that he is not, what no man ever was, incapable of being mistaken. In short, it is more merit, and an argument of a more excellent mind, for a man freely to retract when he is in the wrong, than to be overbearing and positive when he is in the right.*

A man, then, must be willing to know himself, before he can know himself. He must open his eyes, if he desires to see; yield to evidence and conviction, though it be at the expense of his judgment, and to the mortification of his vanity.

CHAPTER VI.

To be sensible of our false knowledge, a good step to self-knowledge.

VI. "WOULD you know yourself, take heed and guard against false knowledge."

See that the "light that is within you be not darkness;" that your favourite and leading principles be right. Search your furniture, and see what you have to unlearn. For oftentimes there is as much wisdom in casting off some knowledge which we have, as in acquiring that

* "If any one can convince me that I am wrong in any point of sentiment or practice, I will alter it with all my heart. For it is truth I seek; and that can hurt nobody. It is only persisting in error or ignorance that can hurt us."—*M. Aurelius*

which we have not; which, perhaps, was what made Themistocles reply, when one offered to teach him the art of memory, that "he had much rather he would teach him the art of forgetfulness."

A scholar, that hath been all his life collecting of books, will find in his library, at last, a great deal of rubbish; and, as his taste alters, and his judgment improves, he will throw out a great many as trash and lumber, which, it may be, he once valued and paid dear for, and replace them with such as are more solid and useful. Just so should we deal with our understandings; look over the furniture of the mind; separate the chaff from the wheat, which are generally received into it together; and take as much pains to forget what we ought not to have learned, as to retain what we ought not to forget. To read froth and trifles all our life, is the way always to retain a flashy and juvenile turn; and only to contemplate our first (which is generally our worst) knowledge, cramps the progress of the understanding, and is a great hinderance to a true self-knowledge. In short, would we improve the understanding to the valuable purposes of self-knowledge, we must take as much care what books we read, as what company we keep.

"The pains we take in books or arts, which treat of things remote from the use of life, is a busy idleness. If I study," says Montaigne, "it is for no other science than what treats of the knowledge of myself, and instructs me how to live and die well."—*Rule of Life.*

It is a comfortless speculation, and a plain proof of the imperfection of the human understanding, that, upon a narrow scrutiny into our furniture, we observe a great many things which we think we know, but do not; and a great many things which we do know, but ought not; that of the knowledge which we have been all our lives collecting, a good deal of it is mere ignorance, and a good deal of it worse than ignorance; to be sensible of which, is a very necessary step to self-acquaintance. See part i, chapter xiii.

CHAPTER VII.

Self-inspection peculiarly necessary upon some particular occasions.

VII. "Would you know yourself, you must very carefully attend to the frame and emotions of your mind under some particular incidents and occasions."

Some sudden accidents which befall you when the mind is most off its guard, will better discover its secret turn and prevailing disposition, than much greater events you are prepared for. For example,—

(1.) Consider how you behave under any sudden affronts or provocations from men. "A fool's wrath is presently known," (Prov. xii, 16,) that is, a fool is presently known by his wrath.

If your anger be soon kindled, it is a sign that secret pride lies lurking in the heart, which, like gunpowder, takes fire at every spark of provocation that lights upon it. For whatever may be owing to a natural temper, it is certain that pride is the chief cause of frequent and wrathful resentments: for pride and anger are as nearly allied as humility and meekness. "Only by pride cometh contention," Prov. xiii, 10. And a man would not know what mud lay at the bottom of his heart, if provocation did not stir it up.

Athenodorus, the philosopher, by reason of his old age, begged leave to retire from the court of Augustus, which the emperor granted him; and as Athenodorus was taking his leave of him, "Remember," said he, "Cesar, whenever you are angry, you say or do nothing before you have repeated the four-and-twenty letters of the alphabet to yourself." Whereupon Cesar, catching him by the hand, "I have need," says he, "of your presence still;" and kept him a year longer. This is celebrated by the ancients as a rule of excellent wisdom. But a Christian may prescribe to himself a much wiser, namely, "When you are angry, answer not till you have repeated the fifth petition of the Lord's prayer, 'Forgive us our trespasses, as we forgive them that trespass against us;' and our Saviour's comment upon it, 'For if ye forgive men their trespasses, your heavenly Father will also forgive you: but if ye forgive not men their trespasses, neither will your Father forgive your trespasses.'" Matthew vi, 14, 15.

It is a just and seasonable thought of Marcus Antoninus, upon such occasions: "A man misbehaves himself toward me—what is that to me? The action is his; and the will that sets him upon it is his; and therefore let him look to it. The fault and injury is his, not mine. As for me, I am in the condition Providence would have me, and am doing what becomes me."—*Meditations*, book v, § 25.

But still this amounts only to a philosophical contempt of injuries, and falls much beneath a

Christian forgiveness of them; which, as Christians, we are bound to, and which, if we know ourselves, we shall be disposed to. And therefore, in order to a true self-knowledge, we must always take care to examine and observe in what manner we are affected in such circumstances.

(2.) How do you behave under a severe and unexpected affliction from the hand of Providence? which is another circumstance, which, when rightly improved, will help us very much to know ourselves.

If there be any habitual discontent or impatience lurking within us, this will draw it forth, especially if the affliction be attended with any of those aggravating circumstances with which Job's was.

Afflictions are often sent with this intent, to teach us to know ourselves; and, therefore, ought to be carefully improved to this purpose.

And much of the wisdom and goodness of our heavenly Father is seen by a serious and attentive mind, not only in proportioning the degrees of his corrections to his children's strength, but in adapting the kinds of them to their tempers; afflicting one in one way, another in another, according as he knows they are most easily wrought upon, and as will be most for their advantage: by which means a slight affliction of one kind may as deeply affect us, and procure as great an advantage to us, as a much greater of another kind.

It is a trite but true observation, that a wise man receives more benefit from his enemies than from his friends, from his afflictions than from his mercies; by which means he makes his enemies in effect his best friends, and his afflictions his greatest mercies. Certain it is, that a man never has an opportunity of taking a more fair and undisguised view of himself than in these circumstances; and therefore, by diligently observing in what manner he is affected at such times, he may make an improvement in the true knowledge of himself, very much to his future advantage, though perhaps not a little to his present mortification; for a sudden provocation from man, or severe affliction from God, may detect something which lay latent and undiscovered so long at the bottom of his heart, that he never once suspected it to have had any place there. Thus the one excited wrath in the meekest man, (Psa. cvi, 33,) and the other passion in the most patient. Job iii, 3.

By considering, then, in what manner we bear

the particular afflictions God is pleased to allot us, and what benefit we receive from them, we may come to a very considerable acquaintance with ourselves.

(3.) In a time of peace, prosperity, and pleasure, when the soul is generally most unguarded, what is its temper and disposition then?

This is the warm season that nourishes and impregnates the seeds of vanity, self-confidence, and a supercilious contempt of others. If there be such a root of bitterness in the heart, it will be very apt to shoot forth in the sunshine of uninterrupted prosperity, even after the frost of adversity had nipped it, and, as we thought, killed it.

Prosperity is a trial as well as adversity, and is commonly attended with more dangerous temptations. And were the mind but as seriously disposed to self-reflection, it would have a greater advantage of attaining a true knowledge of itself under the former than under the latter. But the unhappiness of it is, the mind is seldom rightly turned for such an employment under those circumstances. It has something else to do; has the concerns of the world to mind; and is too much engaged by the things without it, to advert to those within it; and is more disposed to enjoy than examine itself.

However, it is a very necessary season for self-examination, and a very proper time to acquire a good degree of self-knowledge, if rightly improved.

(Lastly.) How do we behave in bad company?

And that is to be reckoned bad company, in which there is no probability of our doing or getting any good, but apparent danger of our doing or getting much harm; I mean, our giving offence to others by an indiscreet zeal, or incurring guilt to ourselves by a criminal compliance.

Are we carried down by the torrent of vanity and vice? Will a flash of wit, or a brilliant fancy, make us excuse a profane expression? If so, we shall soon come to relish it, when thus seasoned, and use it ourselves. This is a time when our zeal and wisdom, our fortitude and firmness, are generally put to the most delicate proof, and when we may too often take notice of the unsuspected escapes of folly, fickleness, and indiscretion.

At such seasons as these, then, we may often discern what lies at the bottom of our hearts, better than we can in the more even and customary scenes of life, when the passions are all calm and still; and therefore, would we know ourselves, we should be very attentive to our frame, temper, disposition, and conduct, upon such occasions.

CHAPTER VIII.

To know ourselves we must wholly abstract from external appearances.

VIII. "Would you know yourself, you must, as far as possible, get above the influence of external appearances and circumstances."

A man is what his heart is. The knowledge of himself is the knowledge of his heart, which is entirely an inward thing; to the knowledge of which, then, outward things (such as a man's condition and circumstances in the world) can contribute nothing; but, on the other hand, if taken into any consideration, will be a great bar and hinderance to him in his pursuit of self-knowledge.

(1.) Are your circumstances in the world easy and prosperous, take care you do not judge of yourself too favourably on that account.

These things are without you, and therefore can never be the measure of what is within you; and however the world may respect you for them, they do not in the least make you either a wiser or more valuable man.

In forming a true judgment of yourself, then, you must entirely set aside the consideration of your estate and family, your wit, beauty, genius, health, &c., which are all but the appendages or trappings of a man, or a smooth and shining varnish, which may lacker over the basest metal.

A man may be a good and happy man without these things, and a bad and wretched one with them. Nay, he may have all these, and be the worse for them. They are so far from being good and excellent in themselves, that we often see Providence bestows them upon the vilest of men, and, in kindness, denies them to some of the best. They often are the greatest temptations that can put a man's faith and firmness to the proof. Or,

(2.) Is your condition in life mean and afflicted? Do not judge the worse of yourself for not having those external advantages which others have.

None will think the worse of you for not having them, but those who think the better of themselves for having them: in both which they show a very depraved and perverted judgment. These are (τὰ ἐκ ἐφ' ἡμῖν) things entirely without us, and out of our power; for which a man is neither the better nor the worse, but according as he uses them; and therefore you ought to be as indifferent to them as they are to you. A good man shines amiably through all the obscurity of his low fortune, and a wicked man is a poor little wretch in the midst of all his grandeur.*

Were we to follow the judgment of the world, we should think otherwise of these things, and by that mistake be led into a mistaken notion of ourselves. But we have a better rule to follow, to which if we adhere, the consideration of our external condition in life, be it what it will, will have no undue influence on the mind in its search after self-knowledge.

CHAPTER IX.

The practice of self-knowledge a great means to promote it.

IX. "LET all your self-knowledge be reduced into practice."

The right improvement of that knowledge we have, is the best way to attain more.

The great end of self-knowledge is self-government, without which it is but a useless

* "Pigmies are pigmies still, though placed in Alps:
And pyramids are pyramids in vales."
Night Thoughts.

speculation. And, as all knowledge is valuable in proportion to its end, so this is the most excellent kind of knowledge, only because the practice of it is of such extensive use, as hath been already shown.

"Above all other subjects," says an ancient pious writer, "study thine own self. For no knowledge that terminates in curiosity or speculation is comparable to that which is of use; and of all useful knowledge, that is most so which consists in the due care and just notions of ourselves. This study is a debt which every one owes himself. Let us not, then, be so lavish, so unjust, as not to pay this debt, by spending some part, at least, if we cannot all, or most, of our time and care upon that which has the most indefeasible claim to it. Govern your passions; manage your actions with prudence; and where false steps have been made, correct them for the future. Let nothing be allowed to grow headstrong and disorderly; but bring all under discipline. Set all your faults before your eyes; and pass sentence upon yourself with the same severity as you would do upon another, for whom no partiality hath biased your judgment."—*St. Bernard's Meditations*, chap. v.

What will our most exact and diligent self-researches avail us, if, after all, we sink into indolence and sloth? Or what will it signify to be convinced, that there is a great deal amiss in our deportment and dispositions, if we sit still contentedly under that conviction, without taking one step toward a reformation? It will, indeed, render us but the more guilty in the sight of God. And how sad a thing will it be to have our self-knowledge hereafter rise up in judgment against us!

"Examination is in order to correction and amendment. We abuse it and ourselves, if we rest in the duty without looking further. We are to review our daily walk, that we may reform it; and, consequently, a daily review will point out to us the subject and matter of our future daily care. This day (saith the Christian, upon his review of things at night) I lost so much time, particularly at ——. I took too great a liberty, particularly in ——. I omitted such an opportunity, that might have been improved to better purpose. I mismanaged such a duty. I find such a corruption often working; my old infirmity still cleaves to me; how easily doth this sin beset me! O! may I be more attentive for the time to come; more watchful over my heart; take more heed to my ways! May I do so the next day!

"The knowledge of a distemper is a good step to a cure: at least, it directs to proper methods and applications in order to it. Self-acquaintance leads to self-reformation. He that, at the close of each day, calls over what is past, inspects himself, his behaviour and manners, will not fall into that security, and those uncensured follies that are so common and so dangerous." —*Bennet's Christ. Orat.*

And it may not be improper, in order to make us sensible of, and attentive to, some of the more secret faults and foibles of our tempers, to pen them down at night, according as they appeared during the transactions of the day; by which means we shall not only have a more distinct view of that part of our character, to which we are generally most blind, but shall be able to discover some defects and blemishes in it, which, perhaps, we never apprehended before. For the wiles and doublings of the heart are sometimes so hidden and intricate, that it requires the nicest care and most steady attention to detect and unfold them.

For instance: "This day I read an author whose sentiments were very different from mine, and who expressed himself with much warmth and confidence. It excited my spleen, I own, and I immediately passed a severe cen sure upon him; so that, had he been present, and talked in the same strain, my ruffled temper would have prompted me to use harsh and ungrateful language, which might have occasioned a very unchristian contention. But I now recollect, that, though the author might be mistaken in those sentiments, (as I still believe he was,) yet, by his particular circumstances in life, and the method of his education, he hath been strongly led into that way of thinking; so that his prejudice is pardonable; but my uncharitableness is not, especially considering, that, in many respects, he has the ascendant of me. This proceeded, then, from uncharitableness, which is one fault of my temper I have to watch against; and which I never was before so sensible of as I am now, upon this recollection. Learn more moderation, and make more allowances for the mistaken opinions of others for the future. Be as charitable to others, who differ from you, as you desire they should be to you, who differ as much from them; for it may be, you cannot be more assured of being in the right than they are.

"Again: this day I have found myself strongly inclined to put in something by way of abatement to an excellent character given of an absent person by one of his great admirers. It is true I had the command of myself to hold my tongue, and it is well I had: for the ardour of his zeal would not have admitted the exception, (though I still think that, in some degree, it was just,) which might have raised a wrangling debate about his character, perhaps at the expense of my own; or, however, occasioned much animosity and contention. But I have since examined the secret spring of that impulse, and find it to be envy, which I was not then sensible of; but my antagonist had certainly imputed it to this: and had he taken the liberty to have told me so, I much question whether I should have had the temper of the philosopher, who, when he was really injured, being asked whether he was angry or no, replied, 'No; but I am considering with myself whether I ought not to be so.' I doubt I should not have had so much composure, but should have immediately resented it as a false and malicious aspersion. But it was certainly envy, and nothing else; for the person who was the object of the encomium was much my superior in many respects. And the exception that arose to my mind was the only flaw in his character, which nothing but a quick-sighted envy could descry. Take heed, then, of that vice for the future.

"Again, this day I was much surprised to observe in myself the symptoms of a vice, which, of all others, I ever thought myself most clear of, and have always expressed the greatest detestation of in others; and that is covetousness. For what else could it be that prompted me to withhold my charity from my fellow-creature in distress, on pretence that he was not, in every respect, a proper object; or, to dispense it so sparingly to another, who I knew was so, on pretence of having lately been at a considerable expense upon another occasion? This could proceed from nothing else but a latent principle of covetousness; which, though I never before observed in myself, yet it is likely others have. O how inscrutable are the depths and deceits of the human heart! Had my enemy brought against me a charge of indolence, self-indulgence, or pride, and impatience, or a too quick resentment of affronts and injuries, my own heart must have confirmed the accusation, and forced me to plead guilty. Had he charged me with bigotry, self-opinion, and censoriousness, I should have thought it proceeded from the same temper in himself, having rarely observed any thing like it in my own. But had he charged me with covetousness, I should have taken it for downright calumny, and despised the censure with indignation and triumph. And yet, after all, I find it had been but too true a charge. O! how hard a thing is it to know myself! This, like all other knowledge, the more I have of it, the more sensible I am of my want of it."

The difficulty of self-government and self-possession arises from the difficulty of a thorough self-acquaintance, which is necessary to it; I say, a thorough self-acquaintance, such as has been already set forth in its several branches, part i. For, as self-government is simply impossible (I mean considered as a virtue) where self-ignorance prevails, so the difficulty of it will decrease in proportion to the degree in which self-acquaintance increases.

Many, perhaps, may be ready to think this is a paradox, and imagine that they know their predominant passions and foibles very well, but still find it extremely difficult to correct them. But let them examine this point again, and perhaps they may find that that difficulty arises, either from their defect of self-knowledge, (for it is in this, as in other kinds of knowledge, wherein some are very ready to think themselves much greater proficients than they are,) or else from their neglect to put in practice that degree of self-knowledge they have. They know their particular failings, yet will not guard against the immediate temptations to them. And they are often betrayed into the immediate temptations which overcome them, because they are ignorant of, or do not guard against, the more remote temptations, which lead them into those which are more immediate and dangerous, which may not improperly be called the temptations to temptations; in observing and guarding against which consists a very necessary part of self-knowledge, and the great art of keeping clear of danger, which, in our present state of frailty, is the best means of keeping clear of sin.

To correct what is amiss, and to improve what is good in us, is supposed to be our hearty desire, and the great end of all our self-research. But if we do not endeavour after this, all our labour after self-knowledge will be in vain; nay, if we do not endeavour it, we cannot be said heartily to desire it: "For there is most of the heart where there is most of the will; and there is most of the will where there is most endeavour; and where there is most endeavour there is generally most success. So that endeavour must prove the truth of our desire, and success will generally prove the sincerity of our endeavour."—*Baxter.*

This, I think, we may safely say, without attributing too much to the power of the human will, considering that we are rational and free agents, and considering what effectual assistance is offered to them who seek it, to render heir endeavours successful, if they are sincere; which introduces the subject of the following chapter.

CHAPTER X.

Frequent and fervent prayer, the most effectual means for attaining true self-knowledge.

"LASTLY. The last means to self-knowledge which I shall mention is, frequent and devout applications to the fountain of light, and the Father of our spirits, to assist us in this important study, and give us the true knowledge of ourselves."

This I mention last, not as the least, but, on the contrary, as the greatest and best means of all, to attain a right and thorough knowledge of ourselves, and the way to render all the rest effectual. And, therefore, though it be the last means mentioned, it is the first that should be used.

Would we know ourselves, we must often converse, not only with ourselves in meditation, but with God in prayer. In the lowliest prostration of soul, beseeching the Father of our spirits to discover them to us; "in whose light we may see light," where, before, there was nothing but darkness, to make known to us the depth and devices of our heart. For, without the grace and influence of his divine illuminations and instructions, our hearts will, after all our care and pains to know them, most certainly deceive us. And self-love will so prejudice the understanding, as to keep us still in self-ignorance.

The first thing we are to do, in order to self-knowledge, is, to assure ourselves, that our hearts "are deceitful above all things." And the next is, to remember, that "the Lord searcheth the heart, and trieth the reins," (Jer. xvii, 9,) that is, that he, the (Καρδιογνωστης) "Searcher of all hearts," (1 Chron. xxviii, 9,) hath a perfect knowledge of them, deceitful as they are. Which consideration, as it suggesteth to us the strongest motive to induce us to labour after a true knowledge of them ourselves, so it directs us, at the same time, how we may attain this knowledge, namely, by an humble and importunate application to him, to whom alone they are known, to make them known to us. And this, by the free and near access which his Holy Spirit hath to our spirits, he can effectually do various ways; namely, by fixing our attentions; by quickening our apprehensions; removing our prejudices; (which, like a false medium before the eye of the mind, prevent its seeing things in a just and proper light;) by mortifying our pride; strengthening the intellective and reflecting faculties; and enforcing upon the mind a lively sense and knowledge of its greatest happiness and duty; and so awakening the soul from that carnal security and indifference about its best interests, which a too serious attention to the world is apt to betray it into.

Besides, prayer is a very proper expedient for attaining self-knowledge, as the actual engagement of the mind in this devotional exercise is, in itself, a great help to it. For the mind is never in a better frame than when it is intently and devoutly engaged in this duty. It has then the best apprehensions of God, the truest notions of itself, and the justest sentiments of earthly things; the clearest conceptions of its own weakness, and the deepest sense of its own vileness; and consequently is in the best disposition that can be, to receive a true and right knowledge of itself.

And, O! could we but always think of ourselves in such a manner, or could we but always be in a disposition to think of ourselves in such a manner, as we sometimes do in the fervour of our humiliations before the throne of grace, how great a progress should we soon make in this important science? Which evidently shows the necessity of such devout and humble engagements of the soul, and how happy a means they are to attain a just self-acquaintance.

And now, reader, whoever thou art, that hast taken the pains to peruse these sheets, whatever be thy circumstances or condition in the world, whatever thy capacity or understanding, whatever thy occupations and engagements, whatever thy favourite sentiments and principles, or whatever religious sect or party thou espousest, know for certain that thou hast been deeply interested in what thou hast been reading; whether thou hast attended to it or no. For it is of no less concern to thee than the security of thy peace and usefulness in this world, and thy happiness in another; and relates to all thy interests, both as a man and a Christian. Perhaps thou hast seen something of thine own image in the glass that has now been held up to thee; and wilt thou go away, and soon "forget what manner of person thou art?" Perhaps thou hast met with some things thou dost not well understand or approve; but shall that take off thine attention from those things thou dost understand and approve, and are convinced of the necessity of? If thou hast received no improvement, no benefit from what thou hast been reading, read it over again. The same thought, you know, often impresses one more at one time than another; and we sometimes receive more knowledge and profit by the second perusal of a book than by the first. And I would fain hope, that thou wilt find something in this that may set thy thoughts on work, and which, by the blessing of God, may make thee more observant of thy heart and conduct; and, in consequence of that, a more solid, serious, wise, established Christian.

But will you, after all, deal by this book you have now read, as you have dealt by many sermons you have heard? pass your judgment upon it according to your received and established set of notions; and condemn or applaud it only as it is agreeable or disagreeable to them; and commend or censure it, only as it suits or does not suit your particular taste; without attending to the real weight, importance, and necessity of the subject, abstracted from those views? Or, will you be barely content with the entertainment and satisfaction, which some parts of it may possibly have given you; to assent to the importance of the subject, and justness of the sentiment, or the propriety of some of the observations you have been reading, and so dismiss all without any further concern about the matter? Believe it, O Christian reader, if this be all the advantage you gain by it, it were scarce worth while to have confined yourself so long to the perusal of it. It has aimed, it has sincerely aimed, to do you a much greater benefit; to bring you to a better acquaintance with one you express a particular regard for, and who is capable of being the best friend, or the worst enemy, you have in the world; and that is yourself. It was designed to convince you, that, would you live and act consistently, either as a man or a Christian, you must know yourself; and to persuade you, under the influence of the foregoing motives, and by the help of the fore-mentioned directions, to make self-knowledge the great study, and self-government the great business of your life. In which resolution may Almighty God confirm you; and in which great business may his grace assist you, against all future discouragements and distractions! With him I leave the success of the whole; *to whom be* glory and praise for ever!

THE END.

www.ingramcontent.com/pod-product-compliance
Lightning Source LLC
LaVergne TN
LVHW010253110826
845151LV00004B/1458

9781425522872